PARATROOPER PADRE
CHAPLAIN FRANCIS L. SAMPSON

TABLE OF CONTENTS

FOREWORD

CARDINAL'S RESIDENCE
452 MADISON AVENUE
NEW YORK
August 21st,

DEAR FATHER SAMPSON:

I am pleased to know that the letters which were published in The American Ecclesiastical Review under the title "Paratrooper Padre" are to appear in book form. I read them as a serial and am sure that they will be well received when they appear in a book.

Congratulating you on your priestly zeal and soldierly heroism and asking God to continue to bless you and your works, I am

Prayerfully yours in Christ
F. CARDINAL SPELLMAN
Archbishop of New York

REV. FRANCIS L. SAMPSON,
Office of the Catholic Chaplain,
23rd Inf. Reg., 2nd Division
Fort Lewis, Washington

INTRODUCTION

The book market has been flooded with war accounts written from almost every point of view. Brass hats have given the public the "big picture." Their aides have tried to show the human side of the brass hats. Practically every Corps, Wing, Division, and Regiment has a book describing its part in the war. Each campaign, battle, operation, and engagement has been exploited in print with no tactical detail slighted. Ernie Pyle led a host of writers in giving to the public the lowly GI point of view, paying proper tribute to the men who were represented in groups of thousands by tiny removable pins on the operational map, men who had no part in the conduct of the war, except to do the fighting, the sweating, the bleeding, and the dying. Mauldin's "Willie and Joe" and Baker's "Sad Sack," both now in book form, gave some comic relief by holding the mirror up to nature, and making the soldier laugh at the reflection of his own experiences of frustration in the army. Gruesome pictorial books have given to millions a vicarious experience of the sickening sensation of fear and a realistic glance at the ghastliness of the grim years 1937 to 1947 in war-torn countries.

Personal accounts of the war have multiplied until publishers have screamed "Halt!" But still the manuscripts keep pouring in, each with a new angle on the subject, with a new point of view, with the latest statistical data, something on the horrors of Dachau, a revelation of the brilliant tactical strokes of a hitherto obscure general, the mistakes of some great military leader hitherto known as a "hero," scandals in high places, the latest humorous side, the involved diplomatic phase, the ethical aspects, biographical sketches, autobiographical accounts. Generals, privates, war correspondents, Red Cross workers, doctors, patients, ex-Nazis, displaced persons, churchmen, congressional representatives, playwrights, novelists, even poets, have belabored World War II until one would think (and devoutly hope) that the depressing material had just about been exhausted.

What possible excuse can there be then, one might reasonably ask, for another book on the subject, especially a book by a priest whose calling might seem to dictate a more peaceable, more elevating theme? Another question might very logically suggest itself. If a priest is supposed to practice the virtue of humility, how come a Catholic chaplain writes an autobiographical account of war experiences?

In answering the first question I should like to make the observation that a priest sees war from a standpoint different from that of anyone else. He is interested more in what is going on inside men than in what is going on outside them. To him the souls of men are even more involved in combat than their bodies; their spiritual resources are more vital to real success than any material factors. The eternal life of a man is as much at stake there as his physical life, and for many a man the sacraments of Penance and the Holy Eucharist were healing the wounds of his soul, while blood plasma, penicillin, and sulfa were healing the wounds of his body. And it is quite possible that in the Providence of God many a man was better prepared than ever before for death that came, not as a thief in the night, but as the ever-expected guide to his eternal home. As a priest, I write from this point of view, and, I dare say, no one but a priest can do so.

The second question is a bit more difficult to answer. I know a great many chaplains who, from the standpoint of background, experiences, ability, and, certainly, holiness, are far better equipped than I to give to our Catholic people an insight into the army priest's thoughts and reactions in the service and in combat. Unfortunately for all of us, however, very few of these capable men have borne witness in print to their extraordinary experiences.

Like many a GI during the war I wrote in some detail to my family about the experiences we were having. There was never any thought at the time that these letters might one day be published. If there had been I am sure that any small merit these pages may have would have been completely ruined by an attempt to be literary. (The three opening chapters of the book have just been written recently to give a background for the action that follows.) A member of the faculty of Sacred Theology at the Catholic University of America happened to read the letters and asked if I would be willing to allow extracts from them to be published in The American Ecclesiastical Review, in the form of a series of articles under the title "Paratrooper Padre." The articles were favorably received, and I was urged to have them published in book form.

A personal narration of the bit of war against Germany which I saw must necessarily be autobiographical, and so might seem a bit egotistical, because of the predominant use of the first person. If you will remember that no pair of knees ever shook more than my own, nor any heart ever beat faster in time of danger; and if you will keep in mind that it was not only impossible… it was unthinkable to allow fear to control your actions in the presence of those fine boys who fought and died so bravely… if you remember these things you will understand how any priest does what he must do almost automatically, instinctively.

These pages may give you the false impression that combat life is always exciting. As a matter of fact, it is, for the most part, monotonous; and the greatest part of every soldier's job mere routine. I have written down only the interesting incidents, and not bothered about our plan or strategy, what we accomplished or failed to accomplish. There were many days when nothing of interest or import happened as far as the regiment was concerned. These pages give you only the high-lights of my own limited view and experience in the war against Germany.

F. L. S.

PART I: TRAINING

CHAPTER I: PARACHUTE SCHOOL AT FORT BENNING

While we were at chaplain school on the campus of Harvard University, they asked for volunteers for the paratroopers. Like a zealous young business man starting out in a strange town, I was ready to join anything out of a sheer sense of civic duty. Frankly I did not know when I signed up for the Airborne that chaplains would be expected to jump from an airplane in flight. Had I known this beforehand, and particularly had I known the tortures of mind and body prepared at Fort Benning for those who sought the coveted parachute wings, I am positive that I should have turned a deaf ear to the plea for Airborne chaplains. However, once having signed up, I was too proud to back out. Besides, the Airborne are the elite troops of the Army, and I already began to enjoy the prestige and glamour that goes with belonging to such an outfit. I literally basked in the praise bestowed upon me by the other chaplains who didn't know that I had signed up without realizing that I would be required to jump. Had they guessed my predicament, it would have made a great joke, and the whole school would have gotten a big bang out of it. It remained, however, my own deep dark secret until now.

The day I arrived at Fort Benning to begin jump training, I received a wire from my brother in The Dalles, Oregon, stating that my mother was very ill. On my way west I called up from Chicago, only to learn that she had died that day. Her body was brought back to Luverne,

Minnesota, the place of her birth and childhood... the place she always called "home"... the place she loved above all others. My mother had always worked hard — very hard. Dad was the manager of a small-town hotel, and mother took care of the food end of the business, and for years did the cooking. Her life was filled with many worries and heartaches, but she always kept her keen sense of humor and Irish wit. The help and guests of the hotel loved her, for her kind and affable nature made the place a home, rather than a lodging house. With scarcely a wrinkle in her face or a grey hair in her head she looked like a young girl as she lay in her coffin. I recalled how often she had expressed the wish that her hair might turn grey; she wanted to look matronly, like the mother of three grown men. The failure of her hair to turn grey can in no way be attributed to the boyhood behavior of her three sons, for if ever a mother had been given cause for worry, and if worry is truly the requisite for grey hair, then my mother's should have been as white as snow. She had often dwelt on the thought that I would one day say her Funeral Mass, and she had spoken of it in a manner of real anticipation and delight. I suppose only the mother of a priest can understand that.

After the funeral, I prepared to return to the Fort Benning jump school, and I discovered that the prospect of jumping from a plane did not seem nearly as hazardous as it had before my mother's death. I realized then that the great mental hazard in parachute jumping was more the subconscious concern for one's family and dependents, than for one's own safety — not, of course, that the latter was ever absent. This fact has been demonstrated over and over again, and, I think, could be authenticated by almost every parachutist. The wives and mothers of paratroopers suffered more keenly, I am sure, the fearful anticipation of the next jump than did the jumpers. As a matter of fact, the paratrooper gains a certain degree of confidence after several successful jumps that is not shared by those who must wait at the phone for the familiar voice, "Made it O.K., darling. The landing was perfect"; or for the dreaded professional voice, "This is the Fort Benning Station Hospital. Your husband..."

I vowed when I was going through the agony of jump school that I would never say anything good about it. It was even tougher than it was reputed to be. In all fairness, though, it must be admitted that the desired results were actually obtained, and the qualities of physical fitness, determination, and aggressiveness nursed at Benning bore fruit at Bastogne. I shall try in the next few pages to be as objective about the jump school as the memory of my sweating body, bruised skin and bones, aching muscles, abused dignity, and deflated ego will permit. If a note of acidity is detectable in my description of the jump school, I would ask the reader kindly to remember that it is entirely premeditated and intentional.

When I reported in at the school, the adjutant told me that the two previous chaplains to enroll were now in the hospital, one with a broken leg, the other with an injured back. My expression must have been both comic and tragic, for he looked at me and laughed, then said encouragingly, "But three or four chaplains have already gone through the school successfully."

I made a noise in my throat that was meant to be a chuckle, and said with an assurance I was far from feeling, "I guess if they can make it, I can."

The School was divided into four weeks of intensive training called Stages A, B, C, and D. With seventy-seven other officers I reported May first to the chief instructor of A stage. The training was conducted by sergeants who gloried in the fulfillment of a sergeant's dream… to be in a position of authority over commissioned officers. Most of these sergeants were former professional athletes and acrobats. The word and order of a training sergeant was as absolute as any order of a commanding officer to his subordinates. One lieutenant colonel who spoke sharply to a training sergeant and refused to obey the sergeant's orders was made to apologize in the presence of the entire class assembled and was then dismissed from the school. They meant business here; they played no favorites, and any man who failed to fulfill the rugged requirements was washed out. Colonels were dropped as readily as second looeys; doctors and chaplains given the boot as ruthlessly as line officers. Those who failed thereafter spoke of the school in terms of bitterness and hatred; and even those who eventually made the grade would always recall the four eternal weeks with more repugnance and revulsion than pride.

Calisthenics and long runs constituted A stage. I had thought that I was in fairly good physical condition when I arrived at Benning, but the first morning of calisthenics — more than three hours of it — convinced me that I was as flabby and soft as any sergeant major in the Quartermaster Corps. We finished the morning with a forty-minute run under a broiling Georgia sun, leaving almost a fourth of the class stretched out at intervals along the road; some in anger had quit, others ran until physically incapable of going farther, and some were out cold. The "meat wagon" ("ambulance" to the civilian) picked them up. Those who finished the run arrived at the barracks at the stroke of twelve, and drenched in sweat, completely exhausted, tired and worn out even beyond the ability to curse the school, flopped on their bunks, unable to make the effort to go across the road for dinner. Food wasn't interesting. A shower required energy to take off fatigues. We only wanted rest, rest, r e s t. Most of us dozed until they blew that infernal whistle again at one p.m.

The same schedule in the afternoon as in the morning, except with a little judo thrown in, plus several tries at the obstacle course, but always finishing up with the inevitable run. I did rather badly with the calisthenics; could never seem to get the hang of climbing the rope, and the Indian-club exercises left my arms limp and incapable long before the sergeant said "enough." I finally learned to do fifty push-ups, but I was almost the last man in the class to do it. The only thing that kept me from being washed out of A stage was the fact that I never dropped out of a run. The crowded barracks of seventy-eight officers had slipped to a comfortable thirty-eight by the end of the first week. Many of them had quit the first couple of days, but not before telling the sergeants — and everyone else connected with the school — what they thought of it. Only the toughest of the students would sacrifice precious hours of sleep for a movie at night. In the evening after supper saying the Breviary in the quiet of the chapel was restful, but I do hope there is some truth to the old legend about the angels finishing the rosary for those who fall asleep from fatigue while saying it. Mass at six a.m. would begin another day just like the last.

B Stage, the second week of training, was much more interesting. During this stage we employed the many ingenious gadgets designed to simulate parachute jumping. The first prop was the fuselage of a plane whose wings had been taken off. They seated twenty-two of us in it at a time, and we were shown how to stand up properly in a plane, how to hook up the strap that pulls the top off the parachute pack, how to check the equipment of the man in front of you, how to respond to the orders of the jump master, and how to make a proper exit from the plane. We began to get cocky; jumping was going to be simple.

But then they took us to the landing trainer! This is a fiendish device by which the student is hooked up in a jumper's harness attached to a roller that slides down a long incline. At any moment he chooses, and always when you least expect it, the sergeant pulls a lever that drops you to the ground while you are traveling about twenty miles an hour. The idea is to hang on to your risers, duck your head between your knees as soon as you touch the ground, and go rolling along like a ball. Failure to duck quickly enough means that you go sliding along the cinders on your face. If you displeased the sergeant by your performance, he generally made you double-time around the training area several times, holding your risers aloft, and telling everyone what you did wrong. I was given eight laps, and had to shout to every man I passed, "I'm a bad chaplain, I dropped my risers!"

At no time during jump school were we permitted to walk — always double-time. Nor were we allowed to lean against anything, or have our hands in our pockets. For violations of these rules push-ups were the punishment. One morning while a sergeant was giving a demonstration I happened to yawn. "All right, Chaplain, give me fifty push-ups." I got through forty-two and couldn't budge another muscle to save my life. I continued to lie on the ground exhausted, supremely indifferent to the jibes of the sergeant and to the laughter of the other officers.

The mock-up tower was a forty-foot platform with a long cable extending on an incline to a big soft pile of sawdust. After the hook-up to the cable, the sergeant would give the signal to jump. The exit, drop, and the jerk from the cable closely simulated an actual jump. The ride to the sawdust pile was fun. We enjoyed this; at least, we enjoyed it until the sergeant forgot to hook up one of the men and he dropped the forty feet to the ground. The "trainasium" was another of the elaborate props — a forty-foot-high maze of bars, catwalks, ladders, etc. There was only one other in the world like it and that was at the parachute school in Germany. We hoped the Germans had as many accidents on theirs as we had on ours.

The afternoons of B Stage were spent in the packing sheds, where we learned to pack our own chutes. This was supposed to give us confidence in the chutes, but most of us would rather leave the job to a professional packer. Our first five jumps would be made with chutes we packed ourselves. This really worried me, for I had no confidence in the bulging lopsided twisted thing that had taken me an hour and a half to pack. The sergeant told us, however, that you could jump a chute thrown in a barracks bag and it would open. The occasional "streamers" in the preceding classes didn't seem to warrant such confidence.

C Stage and the 250 foot "free towers" were next. We took turns in being hoisted to the top of the tower and released. Floating down from 250 feet is pleasant, but the closer you get to the ground the faster you seem to drop, and the earth seems to be rushing up to meet you... Must remember the proper landing technique — feet a few inches apart, toes pointing down, chin in, hands on risers, body neither tense nor relaxed. The instructor's voice over the loudspeaker from the tower, "Don't stretch for the ground! Make a half turn to the right!" It was too late. I landed like a sack of flour. But the body is a wonderful thing; it can collapse and fold up like an accordian, thus absorbing without injury the greatest part of the shock of a bad landing. I was quite satisfied with myself, even though the instructor was not, for I could get up and haul the chute back to the tower without help. I could speak with the voice of experience to the next fellow in line still sweating out his first drop from the free tower.

There was a young second lieutenant in our class, a Polish lad, who had taken the whole course in stride. He was small... about a hundred and thirty pounds, I'd guess, and the calisthenics and runs had seemed ridiculously easy for him. When given fifty pushups for leaning against a post, he asked the sergeant, "With which hand do you want me to give the pushups?" Most of us could scarcely give fifty with both hands, but he did them with his left hand, and was almost as fresh when he finished as when he began. On Saturday morning at the close of C stage, a two-hundred-pound rugged first lieutenant in charge of the officers going through this stage said that he would like to have the chance of separating the men from the boys in the judo pit; and that if any of us thought that we could stay with him three minutes he'd be glad to give us the opportunity. The young Polish officer stepped out. "I'd like a chance to try, sir." We felt that he had gotten in over his head this time, for the instructor was really clever and fast, and had about seventy pounds advantage. But in less than thirty seconds the instructor was flat on his back. Our morale jumped up a hundred per cent, and the young lieutenant became the hero of the school, for no one, including the sergeant instructors, liked the arrogant instructor of C stage.

Confessions Saturday afternoon and evening were very heavy, for besides the officers' class there was a class of 800 enlisted men prepared to make their five qualifying jumps the following week. Many of the men a long time away from the sacraments began to see the light. I doubt that any Mission could more effectively bring men to a realization of the importance of being in the state of grace than the prospect of a parachute jump. Communions on Sunday were inspiration, and I thought that, if this were the effect of the anticipated jump, then parachuting ought to be mandatory for all young men in the service. It was easy, too, to visualize hundreds of mothers and fathers, wives and sweethearts, brothers and sisters, friends and nuns, each remembering in Communion that morning the intention of some boy who was going to leap from a plane twelve hundred feet above the earth with nothing between himself and destruction but a piece of silk.

Monday morning dawned bright and warm. This was it! In a couple of hours we would be experiencing the grand-daddy of all thrills. We were "sweating the jump out," but we would have been really disappointed had the weather been bad and the jump postponed. Scarcely anyone touched his eggs at breakfast, and the usual jokes, about turning in your chute if it doesn't open and getting a new one, were absent this morning. Even the jump school song, "Gory, Gory, What a Helluva Way to Die," sung to the tune of "The Battle Hymn of the Republic," was neglected. Each man was wrapped in his own thoughts as we marched to the packing sheds to pick up the parachutes we had packed for ourselves. Each of us checked the all-important break cord on his chute over and over again. All sorts of tragic possibilities crowded in on our imaginations as we tried to concentrate on the jump master's instructions. "Don't get excited. Stay cool!" he shouted. "Just remember what you have been taught. Don't stand up before you get the signal; don't crowd towards the door. Follow the man in front of you quickly, but don't go out on his back. Keep your chin in until the chute opens, then check your canopy. If you should happen to have a streamer — you won't, these chutes always open — but if you should have a streamer, just pull your reserve, and throw it away from your body, so you won't get tangled in the suspension lines. Now listen, you men, you're a good class, and I don't think there is a yellow guy here. I don't want anyone freezing in the door, I don't want any quitters! Now put on your helmets and line up."

They divided us up so that one officer would lead each group, or "stick," of ten enlisted men. As I left the officers to join the ten enlisted men in my stick, a lieutenant, who had often said to me that he wished that he had been brought up in some religion, quipped, "I hope your Boss isn't mad at us today, chaplain."

Just before we boarded the plane a little red-headed fellow next to me said, "Father, I was on duty Saturday night and didn't get a chance to go to confession. It's only been a couple of weeks, but I sure would like to go."

"But the motors will start up in just a minute," I replied, "you had better make it snappy." With the rest of the men wondering what was going on he leaned over and whispered in my ear. After the absolution I asked him, "Do you feel better now?"

"Father," he said with a grin, "that was better than a reserve chute."

As the plane taxied across the runway, the men fell silent. The plane picked up speed and everyone's jaw muscles tightened, and, as if to show that it was deliberate, each man adjusted the two chin straps on his helmet. The air became cooler in the cabin, and when the plane had cleared the pine trees at the end of the runway the jumpmaster eased the tension somewhat by walking down the aisle and helping the men loosen their safety belts. He lit a cigarette and we followed suit. The plane circled over the packing sheds, and we saw hundreds of tiny men down there waiting for these planes to dump their human cargo and come back to take them up for the identical insane purpose. Fort Benning looked awfully small from the air; the baseball park resembled a billiard table, and the muddy Chattahoochee seemed tiny enough to step across. I spotted a Catholic chapel, and for a moment in spirit I knelt before the Blessed Sacrament.

"Stand up!" shouted the jump master. He was standing in the open door and the prop blast wrinkled and whipped the skin of his face like a dish towel in the wind. My legs turned to jelly and there were butterflies in my stomach. Why couldn't I have been satisfied in some other branch of the service like the…

"Hook up!" We hooked our snap fasteners onto the cable. "Hand around the inside of the static line just below the snap"… that's right. Dozens of instructions began to race through my head… "jump clear of the door… keep chin in close… don't forget to count… check the canopy… don't forget to count!" They told us that a man could fall all the way to the ground before he knew it, if he forgot to count. I must remember, "Don't forget to count." "Check your equipment!" Each man glanced at the chute of the man in front of him to be sure that it hadn't broken open prematurely.

The last man in the stick called out, "Ten O.K.!" as he slapped the man in front of him.

"Nine O.K."

"Eight O.K." and so on down to myself.

"One O.K. sergeant," I said as the pilot throttled the engines down and the red light just over the door went on.

"Stand in the door!" The jump master stepped aside, and I took his place in the door. The men were pressing against each other. The plane was rocking and losing some altitude. The green light was on.

"Are you ready?"

The men broke the tension with a roar, "All ready!"

"LET'S GO!"

The jump master slapped my leg, and out I went. My exit must have been poor, for the prop blast spun me like a top. Head over heels I went, aware of nothing but my absolute helplessness. I forgot to count. The only rule that I observed was keeping my chin pressed into my chest. It was a good thing I remembered that, for, just as the chute opened with a loud smack jerking me almost into unconsciousness, I felt the sharp sting of the suspension lines strike my face. In a fraction of a second the opening of the chute slowed me down from almost ninety miles an hour to zero. Suddenly everything was quiet and peaceful. This quiet and peace of being alone, suspended between heaven and earth by a beautiful canopy of silk was a pleasant sensation. The thrill was nothing at all like what I had expected. The excitement, nervousness, and tension were gone, replaced by a feeling of great satisfaction and genuine enjoyment. The descent was scarcely perceptible and every second of it was precious. I remember that I had that same feeling once before — as a child when I rode an escalator down a flight in a Minneapolis department store.

As I neared the ground the rate of descent seemed to increase greatly. I grasped my risers, and made half a body turn to get the wind to my back. Then I hit! Something snapped in my leg, and a sharp pain ran up and down my body without seeming to localize. I managed to collapse the chute after it had dragged me for about a hundred feet. For a time, after disengaging myself from the harness, I lay there gasping for breath and thinking, "If this is a broken leg or a banged-up knee, it might give me a chance to back out of this foolish business gracefully. Jumping is a boy's racket, not something for a thirty-year-old man." I got up carefully, tested the leg, and it seemed to respond normally. With a sigh, "Well, I guess I'm just stuck with the paratroops, and nobody to blame for it but myself." But this feeling was to change shortly to great pride in the organization, and to genuine respect and esteem and even love for the men in it.

We carried our parachutes to the waiting trucks. The men were jubilant, all talking at once, and each man describing with great animation every detail of his jump. They were bursting with pride. "How'd you land? I hit like a sack." "What an opening shock... looka here!" proudly displaying the rapidly discoloring riser marks on his shoulders. "Any business for the meat wagon? Was anybody hurt?" "Yeah, the guy who lit next to me landed on his tail; they carried him off on a stretcher." "I'd like to go right up and do it again!" "How about it, chaplain? How'd you land? That makes you a real sky pilot, doesn't it?" It was impossible not to share their good spirits. We sensed too that our mutual experience really made us brothers in the Airborne family. Thereafter, though they would often fight among themselves, paratroopers having trouble with civilians, the law, or with men of other units would just have to yell, "Geronimo," and from every tavern, park, and sidewalk within earshot would come running the men with the parachute wings on their breast. This loyalty caused the Army a great many headaches before it paid off in Normandy, Southern France, Leyte, Holland, Bastogne, and Germany. Now, as we rode back to the sheds to shake the dirt and weeds out of the parachutes, the men broke into their song, "Gory, Gory, What a Helluva Way to Die," finishing strongly on the last phrase, "they poured him from his boots."

By the end of the week we had made the five qualifying jumps, received a certificate to this effect, had the wings pinned above the left breast pocket by the school commandant, and then hastened to acquire the overbearing mannerisms and obnoxious characteristics of pre-combat paratroopers. Jump boots, the unique patch on his cap, and the wings were badges of such distinction that the jumper considered himself outside the law, above observing the customary courtesies toward civilians, and in a position to scorn all other branches of the service. There is no difficulty in distinguishing the paratrooper who has seen combat from the one who has not. Combat was one day to mellow him, and give him a wholesome respect for the foot infantry... like the 28th Division which, though reeling from smashing blows of five converging German divisions, still delayed the enemy long enough for the 101st Airborne to set up their impregnable defense at Bastogne. He never dreamed at Benning that he would one day be rescued by an armored division, the natural enemy of Airborne, which had broken through the encircling German lines. He was even to learn that the Air Corps had its points, as ammunition, gasoline, food, and other essential supplies were dropped just in time to prevent a great disaster for the Airborne. That mission was a mighty expensive one for the C-54 men, as many ships went down in flames.

By that time the paratrooper had seen enough combat really to care what happened to the other fellow. He began to appreciate the necessity of team work with all branches of the service. He might even admit on occasion that the airborne could not win the war alone. Yes, the jump school graduate was a swaggering character, but give him time and he would develop into an efficient soldier with becoming poise and quiet self-assurance and a wholesome respect for the rights of others. One day, after the purgatory of combat, you might even think of him as gentle and kind — if he is not provoked to act otherwise.

CHAPTER II: TRAINING AT CAMP MACKALL

My orders sent me to the 501st Parachute Regiment at this time engaged in training at Camp Mackall, North Carolina. Camp Mackall was the first army camp in the United States to be named after a private, a soldier who had died as a result of a parachute jump during training. I was looking forward with real interest and with a certain degree of trepidation to meeting Colonel Johnson, the fabulous CO of the Regiment. He had left a reputation at the jump school of being the toughest, roughest, and noisiest officer ever to "hit the silk." Lieutenant MacReynolds, a powerfully built ex-prizefighter and for the last six or eight years a career soldier, was the adjutant. This was June 7, and one year later to the day Mac's very promising military career was cut short by a piece of a German 88 shell. Major Julian Ewell, the executive officer, stepped out of his office when he heard us talking and I introduced myself. I liked Ewell from the first moment I met him. Behind his quiet dignity and courteous respect one could sense a depth of resourcefulness, that in later days proved to be even greater than anyone guessed.

Colonel Johnson came in, and the atmosphere of the room was immediately charged with his forceful and domineering personality. He was dressed in a tailored jump suit, and was carrying a long knife in his hand. This was overplaying his character a bit, I thought, but I later learned that he practiced knife throwing for an hour every day.

"Hi ya, fella," he said, "who are you?" Major Ewell introduced me. "Come into my office, chaplain." The colonel led the way. "Have a seat. Tell me, why did you join the paratroops?" Mac-Reynolds had told me that this would be his first question, but even so I was not quite ready for it. I could tell by the way he stuck out his jaw that the answer he wanted was a snarl and something about wanting to get at those dirty —— Nazis and at those lousy slant-eyed ——! and that I wanted to be in the toughest —— —— outfit in the cockeyed army and under the roughest, meanest, hell-bent-for-leather CO in the business and that this outfit was it. I am afraid that my real answer was quite a disappointment.

"Well, sir, they asked for volunteers at chaplain's school." "You're a Catholic priest, aren't you?" he said, "I assume you know your religious business… you fellas always do. I'm not a Catholic, but I think you can do a lot of good for my boys. They need a priest. I like your business of confession. I'm not a Protestant either, but I believe in God, and I believe in Jesus. If you have any problems… any problems at all… come in and see me. If any of my boys are getting a rotten deal, I want you to bring it to my attention. I want you to keep your fingers on the pulse of the Regiment. You will know before I will, if anything goes wrong with morale, and I want you to come in as soon as you see something wrong with it and tell me. I want you to be with the men all the time… on their marches, on their night problems, in the field; jump with them when they have to jump. This is what I expect of a chaplain. This is what I expect of you, if you are going to play on my team, fella. There it is… straight from the shoulder. Whadya say?"

"I'll do my best, sir," was my clever reply.

"MACREYNOLDS," he screamed loudly enough to be heard in the next county.

"Yes, sir."

"Take the chaplain over to meet Chaplain Engel. Then fix him up with quarters." I saluted and the colonel responded with the most vigorous salute I had ever seen.

Chaplain Kenneth Engel, a Methodist, was a very pleasant fellow with a fine sense of humor, and a warm way of greeting you that made you feel that he was sincerely glad to know you. He wore glasses and a moustache. He looked rather frail, an illusion that was dispelled when you saw him handle himself on the football field or the baseball diamond. This was the beginning of a very happy association and genuine friendship. Chaplain Engel always called me "Father," and I liked that. Priests are very reluctant to give up this title in the army for the generic and less significant "Chaplain."

Colonel Johnson had been very fortunate in his selection of officers for his "team." Major Kinnard was the S-3, that is to say, in charge of plans and training. He, like Ewell, his close friend and West Point classmate, was a product of great inherent leadership qualities, superb military training, and an unquestioning devotion to duty, and all of this was brought to a zenith of perfection on the battlefields of Europe a year later. His abilities were not long in being recognized after the first test of combat. Major General Maxwell D. Taylor, Commander of the 101st, took Kinnard from the Regiment, and made him G-3, a full colonel at the age of twenty-seven. Harry Kinnard became a close friend. Kinnard and Ewell looked and acted like cold military machines, but the men of the Regiment sensed in these two a deep concern for them and a genuine interest in their welfare.

It is strange, as I think upon it, that Colonel Johnson, so dynamic himself and with so much color — an extrovert of the extreme type — should have gathered so many men of reflective nature into his Regiment, placing them in key positions. Majors Carrol and Ballard were externally very like Ewell and Kinnard, and, though excellent men personally and fine soldiers, they somewhat lacked an understanding of the needs of the men, particularly spiritual needs. As battalion commanders these two officers failed to give any support to religion, and they frustrated, through indifference rather than opposition, every attempt of Chaplain Engel and myself to get cooperation. Ballard ultimately took over command of the regiment, after Ewell was wounded at Bastogne. (Johnson had been killed in Holland.) Carrol was one of the first men to die in the invasion of France in the early morning of June 6.

Major Braden, executive officer of the third battalion, was one of the finest gentlemen I have ever known in the army, and his strong support of the religious program of the regiment was a real help to Chaplain Engel and myself. Braden was not a well man, despite his six-foot-two beautifully proportioned frame, and after a week of combat his ailment gained a victory over his tremendous will power, forcing him to be evacuated. Bottomly, later to become a major, then a lieutenant colonel, and Allen, who followed a like pattern in promotions, were the typical army disciplinarians of the Regiment. These two men were strongly disliked by the men in garrison, but later, in combat, were to win first their respect then their genuine admiration.

Major Philip Gage was a very good soldier and fair-minded enough to struggle against the anti-Catholic prejudices with which he had been brought up. He married a lovely Catholic girl, and fulfilled his part of the contract to the letter by having his children baptized and educated in the religion of their mother. Now and then, however, he couldn't resist giving us a little dig, like, "Thank God, we have at least kept you Catholics out of the White House." But he was big enough to apologize for that remark in the presence of those who overheard it. Gage lost an arm in Normandy, was captured, then liberated two months later when Patton's armored divisions raced across France.

Major Francis Carrel, of Indianapolis, was the regimental surgeon. No relation to the first battalion CO, he was small in stature, but mighty in many ways. A strict disciplinarian, an excellent surgeon, a man of strong faith in God and deep convictions about the inherent dignity of every human being, he chose his men and officers carefully. He preferred common sense, moral integrity, and strength of character to flashier talents or even to experience. He raised the despised "pill-pushers" of garrison life to the level of being the most admired unit in the regiment during combat. Doc Carrel was wounded in Normandy, but gave himself superficial treatment, and continued to carry on when his evacuation would have been a staggering blow to the Regiment as the wounded kept pouring into the aid station.

Well, these were the field grade officers of the regiment, the framework upon which Colonel Johnson was building his fighting unit; this was the coaching staff of his "team." Each of these men influenced the character of the Regiment, and each contributed a great measure to the qualities they helped fuse into a first class combat organization. To the casual observer the Regiment was just a large edition of Colonel Johnson. It naturally reflected his color and some of his individual characteristics. But to those on the inside, the Regiment was much more than that. Its own personality, formed by a thousand different factors, ultimately became the forceful and unique thing that captured the imagination of its personnel, giving them that much spoken of, most desired, and rarest quality in the service — a real esprit-de-corps.

Of the ten field grade officers in the Regiment not one was a Catholic. At first I wondered whether this was by chance or by design and whether my presence in the regiment was simply a matter of filling a vacancy, or whether the staff really wanted someone to minister to the Catholic personnel. In the months that followed, however, I never detected a trace of discrimination, although, of course, we had our differences in matters of regimental policy affecting the religious and moral life of the men. But even in these instances Chaplain Engel's work was as much affected and his protests as loud as my own.

Camp Mackall had none of the conveniences of a regular army post. The barracks were squat one-storied shelters covered with tar paper. The chapel was no different from the other buildings, except that it had in it a roughly constructed altar and pews capable of accommodating about a hundred men. Chaplain Engel and I sat up all night the first Saturday trying to design a backdrop and canopy for the altar and in general give some semblance of dignity to the chapel. The effect was fairly satisfactory. However, the attendance at the two Masses that first Sunday was not. I realized, of course, that the regiment had been without a Catholic chaplain for a long time, and that many of the men didn't know yet that a priest had arrived. I arranged with Major Kinnard to schedule me for a series of sex-morality lectures to the men during their field problems.

This gave me a chance to introduce myself, to get acquainted with the men, and to remind them of their religious obligations. Attendance at Mass picked up considerably.

I was called over to the hospital one afternoon to anoint a boy who didn't look as if he were going to snap out of heat prostration. He later recovered. His name was Manuel Ortiz, same name as the boxing champion, and I was later to anoint him again in Holland for a wound from which he did not recover. As I was leaving the hospital they were bringing in a young man who looked as though he had caught his hands in a cement mixer. Colonel Johnson was with him, and told me to come along. "He's one of your boys, I think, Chaplain. Name's Butkovich… the best damn demolition man I've got… cap went off in his hands." When we arrived at surgery Johnson grasped the doctor by the shoulder, "Save that boy's hands!" The doctor bent over to examine the patient.

"I can save one of them!"

"Both of them!" Johnson flared, "save both of them, or you'll wish you had!" Whatever may have been this man's weaknesses and eccentricities, and he had a great many of both, I was never to forget his passionate concern for his men. In Holland a year later this concern was to occupy even his last thoughts as he turned to his executive officer and groaned, "Julian, take care of my boys." Death had ridden in on a German mortar shell as the Colonel was examining his front lines along the dikes.

Sergeant Stanley Butkovich, of Peoria, Illinois, always attributed to Colonel Johnson the fact that he has two very useful though badly scarred hands. The poor doctor got no credit at all. Butkovich, a cousin of the famous football Butkoviches of Illinois and Purdue, was one of the toughest and best-liked soldiers in the Regiment. His faith and piety and fine example were worth a hundred sermons. In going into Normandy a bullet went through his leg while he was still in the plane. He jumped in spite of this, gave himself an emergency dressing, did more than a creditable job as a demolition squad leader, and was decorated twice for his extraordinary efforts. If he should happen to read this he would never forgive me had I used the word, "heroism."

Two weeks before we were to leave for maneuvers, Colonel Johnson gave one of his famous speeches to the regiment. In private conversation the CO was called "Jumpy Johnson," not just because he would sometimes make five or six parachute jumps in a single day, but also because of the antics he went through when he made a speech.

"Who's the best?" he screamed.

Everyone of the men and officers yelled back at him, "We're the best!"

"What are we here for?" (He had the loudest voice I have ever heard.)

"To fight!" they roared.

"That's right… to fight!" "Jumpy's" eyes were flashing, and he stuck out his jaw in his own inimitable manner. "Those slant-eyed —— in the Pacific, and those dirty kraut Nazi devils just four thousand miles from here know that's what you guys are here for. They're on top now… it's been easy for them so far. Ya know what the lousy rats are doing? They're poisoning the water in Naples; they're poisoning little kids and wimmin! That little skunk with the moustache knows you're coming; he knows you are out to get him and he's scared of ya!" In a rising crescendo of emotional pitch he screamed, "In just a few more months I'm going over and get him! DO YOU HEAR ME? I'M GOING OVER AND GET HIM,' ARE YOU WITH ME?"

Johnson had actually swayed the men until they were sharing his emotions; they were really visualizing themselves jumping on the Reichstag or on Berchtesgaden.

With the men solidly behind him, the Colonel would then berate them for the high percentage of AWOLs, for venereal cases in the regiment, etc. Then he finished by telling them about the coming maneuvers, and explained that it would be a test of whether they were ready to go overseas. The men were anxious to get overseas, and when "Jumpy" ended his speech with another strong appeal to their emotions, they went back to their barracks to write letters home to their families and to their girls about their great CO and that, "the 501st is the outfit selected by the Army brass to capture Hitler… it is still a military secret, though, so don't tell anyone."

"Geronimo" was the regimental mascot — a cadaverous, bleary-eyed, beer-swilling goat. It was the custom of parachute regiments to get a bit of publicity with pictures of their mascots floating down from the sky under a canopy of silk. The airdale of the 506th regiment had already made half a dozen jumps. Colonel Johnson didn't like the idea of another regiment getting more publicity than the 501st; besides, there would be no non-jumpers in his outfit. So, fit a harness, make a chute, call the photographers, Geronimo is going to jump! But the Airborne is a volunteer outfit, and Geronimo had not volunteered. The plane took eight passes at the field, and each pass found Geronimo fighting a winning battle against four men, each of whom had grasped a leg. They were unable to get him out of the plane. Every time they got him near the door Geronimo turned into a dynamo of energy. Those scrawny legs going like pistons threatened the life and limb of everyone in the plane. Because Geronimo wouldn't jump or be pushed out of a plane the Colonel got a bear cub for a mascot, but the thing was missing before we had it a couple of weeks. Geronimo was reinstated, and the band staged a beer party in his behalf. Later, when we were overseas, the outfit that replaced us at Mackall reported that a large and vicious bear had emerged in early spring from its hibernation under one of the barracks.

One day a young man came to me with a very sad tale. His wife was leaving that evening for home in Michigan. He had been rather cross to her of late, and would like to make it up to her by taking her out to dinner, and perhaps to a show. Unfortunately, however, he was caught short. As a matter of fact he was flat broke. Would I be kind enough to lend him about ten dollars! I would. A couple of hours later I dropped into the non-coms' club as was my custom, and here he was, obviously wrapped around about nine dollars and fifty cents worth of beer. He greeted me with unbecoming familiarity, and with one hand on my shoulder and the other still holding an empty beer bottle, his nose about a half inch from mine, asked me if he hadn't borrowed some money from me. I assured him that he had. He said that he wanted to pay it back, and I told him that that made it unanimous, for I wanted him to pay it back too. He then dug into his pocket and drew out a roll of bills as large as my two fists together. He peeled through the bills until he could find such a low denomination as a ten spot. When the same young man dropped into my office a week or so later, I was ready for him. He was short again, and would I be so kind as to lend him…? I assured him in an unmistakable tone of finality that I would not! Then hesitatingly he drew out a five dollar bill. Would I mind exchanging it for a five spot of my own? "Why?" I asked, "is that one counterfeit?" No, it was O.K… the chaplain might find it hard to understand this, but this is the way it is, etc., etc. It seems that chaplain's money in a crap game is better than a rabbit's foot, and puts just the right "hex" on the dice. (Lest anyone draw any unwarranted conclusions I should like to state that I did not bargain for half the "take.")

About the middle of September we were ready to board the troop trains for the Tennessee maneuver area. We were to leave on a Sunday morning, standard operating procedure for the army. (We always moved on a Sunday morning.) But I had announced the Sunday before that Mass on the day of departure would be at 4:30 a.m., and that meant that the Catholics would have to get up at least half an hour before the rest of the Regiment. I couldn't have blamed them too much had they overslept the hour of so early a Mass, but I was really pleasantly surprised by the way they turned out that morning, a tousle-headed, sleepy-eyed, yawning bunch of boys from almost every state in the Union; and with unlaced shoes and open fatigues they knelt in quiet adoration when the sanctuary bell told them that Christ had come down again from his throne in heaven to be with them. The religion of the GI is basic, fundamental, sincere, lacking many of the artificialities and conventions that civilians are sometimes prone to confuse with essentials. Until I had been in the army for some time I had mistaken their swaggering for arrogance, their weaknesses for maliciousness, their frankness for disrespect. Looking back now I cannot recall a single instance of flagrant intentional disrespect on the part of a GI, although I have come to know thousands, some of whom had never seen a priest before they got into the army, but had heard many a strange story about them.

Next to combat, maneuvers offers the chaplain the best opportunity of studying, understanding, and drawing close to the men. I suppose our Regiment's personnel was like any other's except that the glamor and adventure associated with jumping attract a younger group of men than the average straight infantry. Why had they volunteered for the Airborne? Of course the extra fifty dollars a month was an obvious attraction, and, for some of the older men, the only attraction. But for many of the younger boys, some of whom were well under the proper enlistment age, the boots, the patch, and the wings meant girl-appeal when they went home on furlough. These boys had been high school athletes, gridiron heroes of the local school and home town. This type was used to being singled out of the crowed as quite a somebody, and in the service he wanted a unique branch, a special outfit, something that would capture the imagination of his little brother and the other movie-going kids of the neighborhood.

Then there was the quiet type, the men and boys who accepted the challenge of the Airborne to convince themselves or someone "quite special" that they were not colorless, run-o-the-mill, dependables doomed to a lifetime of mediocrity. This type of man frequently did extraordinary things in combat; he would initiate a spontaneous attack when the others were doubtful; he would volunteer for the most difficult assignments; he would die trying, when he might have lived and not been censured for holding back. This was the stuff of which most of the war's real heroes were made. They had little of the passion of courage and a great deal of the emotion of fear. Their bravery, though, was of the highest kind; they had thought it all out before they ever heard a shot fired in anger, and their actions were willful, deliberate, premeditated.

The outfit also had a fair number of professional thugs and ex-criminals, deliberately put there by the authorities to "blood" the men, to toughen them, to make them killers. This group was a nuisance in garrison, and almost useless in combat. They moaned about the food, were bitter towards all officers, inferred that some officers were going to get a slug in the back in combat; they were habitual AWOLs, and in combat were seldom seen, except when they had a chance to push around a few prisoners. They got the easiest and safest details, for they couldn't be trusted to do their job at the front.

Naturally it is a simple matter to look backward and say that this or that man was a good soldier because he possessed such and such qualities, and that other man was a poor soldier because he didn't have those same qualities. But this is arguing in a vicious circle by indentifying in retrospect the qualities with the success. The actions of men are not that easy to predict, even the actions of the simplest of them. In the test of battle the ex-floor-walker sometimes succeeds where the professional soldier fails, and the ex-prizefighter may run, leaving his buddy, a lad that never got away from his mother's apron strings, to hold the position. It is impossible to foretell with one hundred per cent accuracy what any one man will do under the tension and stress of fire. There are too many undetermined factors and considerations to which the prophet has no access. Chief among these considerations, of course, is the free will. But it stands to reason that the habit of self-control and self-discipline must be already strongly entrenched in a man's character if he is expected to make the honorable choice between duty and self-preservation. Religion alone possesses motives powerful enough to make a man persevere in his efforts at self-control and self-discipline. In other words, religion is the indispensable support of those qualities of heart and mind so necessary for a good soldier. Good soldiers are necessary for a strong army. A strong army is necessary for the preservation of those God-given and inalienable rights which can be lost through weakness. Our American rights then are dependent upon the strength of our religion.

But let's get back to Tennessee. Maneuvers have always bewildered me. I could never figure out the objective, or what the waving of various colored flags could prove about the accuracy of either side's fire, or what was gained by tagging a man as wounded, putting a splint on his leg and sending him back to the rear only to have him show up in his company again within the hour. We moved quickly at times, usually at night, and I never could be sure just where we were or where we were going. I almost flunked the map-reading course at chaplain's school, so all I needed to get completely lost was a good map and a compass. These excursions in the dark, though, were very handy for falling in with some fellow who hadn't been to the sacraments in a long time and getting him to go to confession. The attendance at Mass and the reception of the sacraments on maneuvers was much better than in garrison. There is something inspirational about saying Mass in the open using a jeep as an altar, and you feel a kinship with the priests of the primitive Church when you hear confessions while seated on a tree stump.

"Chicken Hill" was a spot that none of the old 501st troopers will ever forget. We were bivouacked for a few days on the side of the hill just above a small chicken farm. The ever-hungry GIs relieved the poor farmer of just about all of his three or four hundred chickens in the first couple of nights. "Jumpy" Johnson made one of his famous speeches then, and deducted twelve cents from the pay of every officer and enlisted man to pay for the chickens.

I had missed dinner one day, and decided to go foraging for myself. The wives of Tennessee farmers were wonderful cooks, and they would receive hungry soldiers into their houses to have a bit of breakfast of pork chops, fried potatoes and gravy, apple sauce, soda biscuits, etc. When the soldier would ask how much it would be, the lady of the house would blushingly suggest, "Is twenty-five cents too much?" With this sort of a meal in mind I approached a farm house, but first happened to look toward the barn. A couple of GIs with their heads stuck around the end of the barn were motioning me to come. They had two nice chickens roasting above a slow fire. They were about clone and smelled wonderful.

"Is there anything wrong with taking just two little chickens from a guy that has so many?" they asked.

"Well," I pondered, "it isn't exactly right according to the law of God or man; but, now if you were to share with a hungry man of religion… We ate them right down to the last neck, and chicken never tasted so good. When we finished I suggested, of course, that we ought to pay for them. The boys felt that was right. They didn't mind paying for the chickens after eating them, for they had little chance to spend their money while on maneuvers anyway, but they wouldn't have liked paying for them before. Snitched chicken always tastes better. We each threw in a dollar, and one of the boys went up to the house.

"How much for your chickens?" he asked the farmer.

"Reckon about a dollar apiece."

"Here's three dollars." He handed the farmer the money and started to walk away.

"Wait a minute, young feller, and I'll get you the chickens," the farmer called.

"That's O.K., we've et two of them already. You can eat the other one... a chicken dinner on us."

At first, time passed very rapidly on maneuvers. Each problem lasted five days. Saturday and Sunday afternoons the men were allowed in Tullahoma to take a shower, to see a movie or to watch the local Military Academy play football, to flirt with the local belles, and some of them to harass the civilians and police. But after about six weeks we began to tire of maneuvers; we were tired of training. All of us wanted to get home for a few days, and then get overseas to finish up this war business in a hurry (it just couldn't last long after we got into it!). When men begin to feel a sense of uselessness, as we were beginning to feel, having had no real part in the war, morale goes down, men become very difficult to control and they seek refuge from their boredom in drink or something worse. So strong disciplinary measures become necessary, and then morale really scrapes bottom. "Jumpy's" speeches began to fall flat. The men had matured; they began to resent the pep-rally tactics of the Colonel, and were embarrassed by the jibes of other troopers levelled at the famous antics of the CO. On one occasion, when he sought to rouse the men emotionally he got no response. When he screamed, "What are we here for?" instead of answering with the customary "To fight!" the men roared back at him,

"FURLOUGHS!" Colonel Johnson was desolate — desolate and scared. He was scared now that, if the brass in Washington failed to send the outfit overseas soon, the keen edge of this great weapon honed by superb training and leadership would be dulled by apathy and indifference.

Short furloughs had been granted as soon as we returned from Tennessee. Before some of the men were back wires had to be sent ordering them to return at once to Camp Mackall. Word had finally come! We were to leave almost immediately! Then came the turmoil of packing; personal affairs had to be cleared up; everyone had a thousand and one things to do, some of which were army duties, others each man's own private concern. It had come down by the grapevine that New York was the port of embarkation designated for the 501st. When we boarded the troop trains and headed north we were sure the "big town" was our goal. But the train didn't even stop in New York, and literally hundreds of wives and sweethearts were left waiting at pre-arranged spots in that city for the boys who didn't show up. Many of the men were furious as they watched the towering skyscrapers recede into the haze of Manhattan twilight. It turned out that Boston was the port from which we departed upon the great adventure. How long till we would see these blessed shores again, and how many of us, we wondered as our ship left the famous Boston harbor behind and pushed its way into the inky waters of the Atlantic, would perhaps, never live to breathe again the free air of America?

CHAPTER III: THE YANKS IN ENGLAND

The rugged Scottish landscape seen through the fog from the ship's deck in early morning is really impressive; it is virile, invigorating, energizing. It is the sort of country bound to produce such literature as the Waverley Novels, and the vigorous writings of such men as Stevenson and Burns. We hugged the coast for several hours, and everyone of us was enjoying this part of the trip immensely. We disembarked at Glasgow, and were treated to a "spot of tea" by a very cheerful group of Scotch Red Cross lassies. The trains we then boarded seemed obsolete, with their worn-out mohair seats, cracked windows unreplaced, and the unsociable (from the American's point of view) private compartment system. We were to learn to respect the English railroads, however, for the speed of the trains and their punctuality made travel there easy and pleasant.

Trucks carried us from a station just outside of Newbury, Berkshire, through this pleasant little city of fifty thousand inhabitants, and to the tented area that was to be our home until "D Day" and again for a while after we returned from Normandy until we jumped into Holland. The streets and sidewalks of Newbury were narrow, and the shops were small, and the GIs got a big wallop out of the signs: "Cinema," "Chemist," "Fruiterer," "Pub." Little boys ran along side the trucks calling out, "Any gum, chum?" "Got a penny?" A GI scarcely ever failed to toss something, and usually felt worse than the child if he had nothing to give. The local citizens seemed very friendly; they smiled and waved, and even the girls didn't seem to mind being whistled at any more than American girls did. All the Americans were overdoing the broad "a," and everybody was "old chap" or "old bean" and was "jolly well glad to be in deah old England, don'tcha know."

Merry England really was merry that first night. The GIs were happy, and they could scarcely wait to get their wrinkled but clean ODs out of their barracks bags, walk the two miles to town, look around, maybe meet some girls and see a cinema, and best of all, see what the inside of a pub was like. The excitement of these novelties was soon to wear off and would be replaced by an uneasiness. This uneasiness was caused by the fact that just twenty miles of English Channel separated us from the Germans, and we knew that we would be crossing that Channel before many months had passed.

Before we pitched into training in earnest we were given a few days to orient ourselves, to shake the salt of the ocean off our boots and in short to visit London. It wasn't long before Charing Cross, Piccadilly Circus, Oxford Circus and numerous other focal points of the second largest city in the world became as familiar to us as New York's Time Square, Riverside Drive and Hell's Kitchen, as the Mall in Washington, as Canal Street in New Orleans, as Market Street in San Francisco, or as familiar as Main Street in Redfield, South Dakota. The GIs took England by storm. There were now a million of them in that little country, each with fifty bucks every month which he was determined to spend on anything that offered a little diversion. The English were startled by the wanton display of so much money for entertainment, and the British serviceman quite understandably resented the advantage the American had over him when it came to getting a date. Street fights between the servicemen of the two countries were common. I had always thought that some American soldiers must be the most profane and vulgar-speaking in the world, but I soon discovered that they can't hold a candle to some British soldiers or civilians.

Major General William Lee, Commanding General of the 101st Airborne Division to which we were now attached, gave a talk to the regiment that inaugurated the intensive training program. This talk was the finest Christian analysis I have ever heard of the purpose of an army, of the dignity of the soldier's profession, and of the high standard of deportment and of personal integrity rightly expected of every man who had been given the opportunity of wearing his country's uniform. These were sincere words from a deeply sincere man. To this man soldiering was not just a career — it was a vocation; a total dedication like the priesthood. He told us what lay ahead, and that sacrifice and obedience to an heroic degree would be required of us. The enlisted men and officers alike were profoundly moved, perhaps as much by the greatness of the man as by what he said. There was no shouting at this speech, but when it was over every man returned to his duties a better soldier. Confused minds began to see a break in the clouds.

A couple months after this talk Bill Lee, as everyone referred to the general, had a heart attack and had to go to the hospital. Sheer exhaustion and physical disability could never have kept him in bed; he had to be confined there by order of his superiors. I had contracted a touch of the flu at this same time and had a room across the hall from General Lee's room. I made bold one day to rap on his door. Obeying a pleasant, "Come in," I enquired how he was feeling. After that, each day he would tell the nurse to invite me in for a short visit. A monk could not have more cheerfully resigned himself to his ailment than this man, who loved the title "soldier" more than "general." Lee was replaced by a younger, more vigorous, perhaps more brilliant man, General Maxwell D. Taylor, who probably excelled his predecessor in every respect but greatness. Taylor was one of the most successful young generals of this war, and now occupies the very responsible position of Superintendent of the United States Military Academy at West Point. Less than a year before taking command of the 101st lie had given real proof of the promise of his meteoric military career when he parachuted alone behind the German lines in Italy, and, under the very noses of the Nazis, met and obtained from Marshal Badoglio a declaration of Italian non-belligerence.

Training in England was a real hardship for everyone. The weather from January, when we arrived there, till June was cold and drizzly. Our field problems were long and difficult. Jumping-in England was extremely hazardous. In North Carolina the heat waves thrown up by the warm sand had made parachuting fairly easy, and the sand also cushioned the shock of the landing. But the atmosphere in England was very thin, making the descent faster, and the rocky soil, numerous fences, and the omnipresent hedge-rows were added hazards that we were not accustomed to. Besides this, we jumped with more equipment and were more heavily weighted down than ever before. The injury casualties were very high, about ten per cent, whereas they had been less than two per cent in North Carolina. On one night jump I lit in a tree and cracked a couple of ribs against the trunk. Night jumping from then on held real terror for me.

After four or five jumps in England it was decided to risk no further casualties, for such highly trained and specialized troops were very difficult to replace.

On one of our night problems the battalion to which I had attached myself was to jump, assemble, and then work its way toward the village of Lambourne. A road-block was to be set up outside the town, we were to dig in, wait for a couple of hours, then attack and take Lambourne just before dawn. After the road-block had been set up, being very tired, I lay down in a ditch beside the road, pulled my trench coat tight around me, and went to sleep. I don't know how long I had slept when I awoke feeling something cold and flat pressing under my chin. Fearful that it was a snake I opened my eyes slowly. It was a long knife blade so sharp that I was almost afraid to breathe. "Chaplain," whispered Colonel Johnson menacingly, "in combat you would have been a dead duck by now."

About seven miles north of Newbury was a lovely residential district called Coldash. The Franciscan Missionaries of Mary, a wonderful order of sisters, had an orphanage there. All the orphans were girls except two little boys who stuck to each other like Siamese twins. The Catholic chaplains located in this section of England met at Saint Gabriel's Home for Children once a month, and these meetings were to be among my most pleasant recollections of England. For a couple of hours we would have a conference to discuss any problems that we might be having in our units. The sisters then served a dinner that made us forget for the time being that there had ever been a shortage of food in England. The sisters worked their own farm, however, and the healthy applecheeked orphans, many of whom were children of people killed in the bombings, were at least spared the most dreaded aspect of war, hunger and starvation. After dinner the children would put on a little show, and they really were clever. They sang mostly American songs, and always closed with a rousing "Gawd bless Awmerrricaw, lawnd of the frrrrree."

I had just finished visiting our sick men in the hospital one afternoon when a call came through requesting a priest. Two badly burned young men were being brought in an ambulance from the scene of an accident. It seemed that their gasoline truck had blown up, and they had both asked for a priest. When they arrived I could see at once that one of them had not long to live; the other was not in too serious a condition. I asked the seriously burned lad if he wanted to go to confession.

"No, Father," he said, "I went Saturday and everything is O.K." He said an act of contrition and I gave him absolution, then anointed him and said the prayers for the dying. As the doctor and nurses covered his body with oil, the boy kept saying over and over again well-practiced ejaculations, "My Jesus, have mercy on me. Mary, help me. Saint Joseph, pray for me." When the doctor left, one nurse remained to drop a little water now and then on her patient's parched tongue.

"Son," I said, "you may die. We all have to die someday, and I only hope when my time comes that I will be as ready as you are now. Shall we say the acts of Faith, Hope and Charity together?" He said these prayers without hesitation or help from me, and, as he continued to repeat them, the nurse, a very young girl with probably little experience, began to cry. The dying boy noticed her crying, looked up at me, winked, and with just a trace of a smile on his face he closed his eyes and died.

Since the regiment was split up in two different areas several miles apart, I arranged to have the Catholics transported by truck each Sunday for Mass in Newbury. They liked Mass in a church for a change, and I was happy to have the opportunity of singing a High Mass each Sunday, a rare privilege for the average army chaplain. Canon Green, a venerable eighty-year old gentleman, was the pastor, and he dearly loved to preach to American GIs… "our gawllant American allies" as he called us.

My evenings were kept pretty well occupied by instructions. Many men were becoming very interested in the Church, not just because they had any premonition of disaster, but principally because when men live together for long periods of time they get to speaking their inmost thoughts, their secret desires, their fears, their anxieties, their unanswered questions about religion, their sense of confusion about life's meaning and its basic problems. Here and there a Catholic man had given a fine example and had been articulate enough to some buddy of his to convey the idea that the Catholic Church had the right answers. Instructions were streamlined to three per week for a period of two months. The correspondence course of the Confraternity Home Study Service was a great help. When I had finished the instructions and was morally sure that the catechumens were sincere and intended to live good devout Catholic lives I would take them up to Saint Gabriel's for baptism. After the baptism, I celebrated Mass, and the newly baptized and their godfathers received Communion. There were usually six to ten in a class, and the sisters always had a good dinner set for them after Mass. Then the kids would put on their show. Even if there were only two baptized, the performance had to take place… the children insisted on it, and the GIs loved it.

Confirmations were also held at Saint Gabriel's for the American soldiers in the area by the bishop of the local diocese. He was a very kindly man.

I would frequently take a group of men up to the orphanage on Sunday afternoons. It is difficult to say whether the soldiers enjoyed the kids more than the kids enjoyed the soldiers, but these excursions were mighty popular affairs. Each child adopted a couple of soldiers to pray for them when they would be in battle. Later, when we were in Normandy and Holland, letters, some of them just a child's scrawling and drawing, from their little friends in Coldash brought grins to the faces and a warm glow to the hearts of these hard-boiled paratroopers. There was more than one soldier buried with the letter of an orphan of Saint Gabriel's still in his breast pocket. And whether their soldier lived or died, I know that God heard and answered the prayers of these little ones in His own way.

"Mouse" Rapp, a Medic, had had quite a career for a little fellow who had just turned twenty-one. He had quit high school in his sophomore year, become an acrobat in a carnival, switched to a tumbling act in the Pantages circuit, then to master of ceremonies in a Chicago burlesque, and finally gave that up to work in a pet hospital for a man who practically adopted him. He was one of the most valuable men in the regiment, even if he had never bound a wound, or fired a shot, or done a day of KP, for "Mouse" was what is commonly known as a "screwball," and he did more for the outfit's morale than all the high-salaried and often smutty professional entertainers who were sent to us.

One evening Mouse and I were going to the cinema in Newbury, and were queued up in line to buy our tickets. A very attractive English girl was standing directly in front of Mouse, and he kept making remarks about her cute hat. The girl had given him several icy but ineffective looks before she turned to me.

"Does that belong to you?" she asked, with a contemptuous nod toward my companion. That was all that Mouse needed.

"Father," he said, "you wouldn't want to sit next to me in the movie. I munch popcorn and crack my knuckles during the exciting parts. But now, if this young lady would just let me buy her ticket and sit next to her I'd be as quiet as a mouse, I betcha." The girl's native reserve broke a bit and she smiled. Today Henry Rapp and Mary, his lovely English wife, are living in Wayzeta, Minnesota, and, if your travels ever take you by that beautiful little suburb of Minneapolis, stop by at the Deep Haven Kennels and ask to see the manager... everyone calls him "Mouse." He and Mary will be glad to see you, and you will be glad you stopped to meet them; everyone likes Mouse and Mary.

The Benedictines had a tremendous monastery about fifteen miles north of Newbury, and operated a splendid boys' school there. American chaplains were always welcome, and frequently we brought out groups of our own men to enjoy the very pleasant atmosphere of the place, to watch the monastery boys play cricket, and once in a while to put on a demonstration baseball game for the monks and the boys of the school. The Americans couldn't understand the quiet studious deportment of the cricket players in action, and were more than amazed to see the two teams calmly lay down their equipment at four p.m. to go have tea even though the score at the time was tied. No amount of explaining by the English boys during tea could justify such procedure in the minds of the Americans. By the same token the English boys and monks were completely bewildered by the steady line of chatter of the American players during the baseball game, and were shocked beyond words by the way one side or the other always challenged the decision of the umpire on every close play, and by such Brooklynese expressions as "Trow da bum out," "Why doncha get some glasses," "We was robbed," etc. I suppose they may have been especially shocked because I happened to be the unfortunate umpire.

Sunday, May 11, was Mothers Day, and we prepared to hold a Solemn Field Mass for all the soldiers stationed around Newbury. I asked the Abbot of the monastery if he would be kind enough to allow the boys choir to sing. He consented. The setting of the Mass was beautiful, and besides twelve hundred GIs about two hundred English attended. Fr. Fitzgerald, C.S.C., preached the finest sermon on motherhood that I have ever heard. After the Mass I took the choir boys to the Officers' Mess for a big chicken dinner.

About two weeks before D Day I had a chance to get up to Oxford, and I took a tour about the University. It was very different from American universities, but I really was impressed, and enjoyed seeing Campion Hall, though its famous rector, Fr. D'Arcy, S.J., was away giving talks somewhere.

The atmosphere in England toward the end of May was getting tense. The big day couldn't be very far away. The war room at division headquarters was under double guard; airfields were beehives of activity; long convoys of trucks were heading for the southern ports of the isle; we had the most realistic dry run yet, traveling to the airfields in trains, loading the planes and boarding them fully equipped. Rumors were flying around fast, and The Stars and Stripes carried the story of a major general who had been demoted to lieutenant colonel because he hazarded a guess in public as to when D Day would be. But the sure sign, in the mind of the GI, that the real thing was not far away was the buddy-buddy attitude of the officers toward their men. Censorship of mail became stricter than ever, as the GIs' letters became longer and more serious. Mass was better attended, and some long-timers were getting back to the sacraments. The men had been well trained; they had confidence in the regiment's leadership and in their own ability. We were ready... as ready, we felt, as we ever would be.

PART II COMBAT

CHAPTER IV: THE INVASION OF NORMANDY

There would be no mistaking the meaning of the elaborate preparations this time. This wasn't a dry run. They don't pass out "live" ammunition for a dry run. About ten days before the invasion two battalions of the Regiment were sent to Merry-mount Airport, the third battalion to the Airport just outside of Reading, almost a hundred miles away. The men were not allowed to leave the tent area within the field, except to march in companies to the war rooms, where everyone was briefed on the mission. The closest possible guard and secrecy were observed; there was a double check of all passes. The band, which, of course, was not going with us, outdid itself with its music to keep the morale up. There was no KP or other onerous duties either; a colored service unit took care of that. The men were in high spirits as they sat in the sun outside their tents sharpening their knives or writing letters home, or just swapping stories. They were confident. They were the best! Colonel Johnson had told them they were for more than a year now, and they had come to believe it. As General Eisenhower passed among the men with his friendly grin and informal chats, it is difficult to say whether he gave them more confidence than they gave him as they grinned back. He was the GI's "right guy," and refused to show in his face the terrific burden of the decision for which he accepted full responsibility, nor did he betray a certain apprehension he must have felt.

Arrangements were made for Chaplain Engel and myself to fly back and forth between the airports, so that we could see all of our men before D Day and H Hour. I had each man write his name and put it in a box beside my tent when he went to confession, so that I might be able to check up later to make sure all the Catholic men got to the sacraments. Though the confessions took more than three afternoons, it was a real satisfaction to know that all of the Catholics of the Regiment had fortified themselves in the sacrament of Penance. It took almost an hour to distribute Communion at the Mass on the eve of departure.

General Taylor gave an inspirational talk, but like so many general officers who lose contact with the average soldier's mentality, he used the expression "our glorious mission" and referred to the fact that within twelve hours we would be "making history." The average soldier sees nothing glorious in killing a farmer's son, mechanic, a school boy, or a laboring man, even if those individuals do happen to be in the German army. Many of the GIs had read too much history to take pride in being a part of its most sordid aspect. Such high flown phrases as "glorious mission" and "making history" irritated the average American soldier, and later, after the blood bath of battle in which he saw his buddies wounded, mangled, dead, after the excitement had worn off and the feeling of futility had set in he was to recall these phrases with bitterness. No one knows better than a soldier that war is a filthy, rotten, loathsome thing, and for him it can never be dolled up with words to be anything else. He does his job well because that is the quickest way to get the hateful ordeal over with.

After the General, Colonel Johnson gave his talk. It was a talk he had looked forward to since the war began, a talk that I am sure he had rehearsed for months. He used his time-honored tactics and they were effective. The men responded; they knew their CO had guts, a quality they admire in an officer above tactical ability. At the emotional peak of his talk "Jumpy" reached for his knife which was strapped to his boot. He had some rather embarrassing difficulty getting it out of its case, but when he finally did he raised it high above his head and screamed, "I swear to you that before the dawn of another day this knife will be stuck in the foulest Nazi belly in France! ARE YOU WITH ME?"

"WE'RE WITH YOU."

"THEN LET'S GET 'EM! GOOD HUNTING!"

Colonel Johnson jumped down from the stand, and we went to put on our equipment, and to make any last minute adjustments of parachute harnesses. We were much over-equipped, the fault, we suspected, of some logistics expert in the Pentagon, who tested his theories by jumping off a footstool fully equipped. Most of us with our equipment weighed well over three hundred pounds, and I recalled that I had blown a couple panels from my chute in jump school with only my own hundred and eighty pounds exerting the pressure.

As we marched to the planes I waited as the men went by and shook each man's hand and gave him a sincere "God bless you!" After boarding the planes I led our plane load in a short prayer. We took off on the second and once the formations had formed we went at top speed. The boys were rather quiet; some tried to sleep, others smoked steadily, and a few tried to be nonchalant by singing some modern songs. I was wondering if we would meet any fighter planes over the Channel… it was a cold night and the Channel water is always like ice… I didn't relish an emergency jump. We got across without mishap and only one enemy plane came near us. But, as soon as we were over land the ack ack was terrific. The plane was hit many times and one boy had a bullet go right through his leg. As we stood up and hooked up, the plane was rocking badly in a strong wind. The green light came on and the jump master pushed our equipment bundle out and we went out as fast as we could, my assistant right behind me. Our jump was a surprise all right... for us! The Germans were waiting for us and they sent such a barrage of bullets at us that it will always remain a mystery to me how any of us lived. The tracer bullets alone made it look like Fourth of July. I collapsed part of my chute to come down faster. From there on my guardian angel took over.

I lit in the middle of a stream over my head. I grabbed my knife and cut my bags from me (my Mass kit, etc.) but could scarcely move to free myself. The canopy of my chute stayed open and the strong wind blew me down the stream about 100 yards and into shallow water. I lay there a few minutes exhausted and as securely pinned down by equipment as if I had been in a strait jacket. None of our men was near, and it took about twenty minutes to get out of my chute (it seemed a year, with German machine gun and mortar fire sweeping the area). I crawled back to the edge of the stream near the spot where I landed, and started diving for my Mass equipment. By pure luck I recovered it after the fifth or sixth dive. The whole area was swamp, and as I started getting my bearings I looked for the lights to assemble on. I learned later that they were shot out as soon as they were turned on and the men in charge mostly killed or wounded. Very luckily I spotted my assistant not very far away, still struggling to get out of his chute. We got together and made for the nearest hedgerow that would offer cover. We no sooner got there than a plane on fire came straight at us. The plane crashed about eighty yards in front of us and threw flaming pieces over our heads. We saw two more planes go down not far away. Neither of us had a weapon so we welcomed two of our men who came crawling along the hedgerow.

Our little group got together and started toward the place we judged our troops might assemble. We moved slowly under concealment of hedgerows, and welcomed the sight of half a dozen paratroopers running down the road ditch. They were not of our Regiment but told us where we might find the 501st or a part of it. We went in the direction they pointed until we came under heavy enemy rifle fire and I approached a nearby farmhouse. I walked in and found the house full of wounded paratroopers… about twenty-five of them. It was just a three room house and the French farmer, his wife and child were there. Chaplain McGee — a splendid Protestant chaplain — was giving first aid as best he could. He had run out of bandages and since I, my assistant, and the Medic were well supplied he was very happy to see us. We all worked with the men for the better part of the day. A boy came in wounded telling us of his buddy who was shot in the back in the tall weeds about 100 yards from the house. Chaplain McGee and I decided to try and find him. Just as we stepped out of the house (front door) a German mortar hit the back door and killed the French woman and the little girl. The poor farmer nearly went out of his head.

About six p.m., some of the patients getting worse, I decided to try to find a doctor, so I went looking for our Regimental Aid Station. I left my assistant with Chaplain McGee. After going about a mile I found a patrol of our men and they told me where to go. Since the area was under fire I avoided the road and went by way of the swamp. The deep swamp was filthy and cold but afforded good cover. I finally reached the Regimental Aid. There was quite a fight going on there. The enemy had dug in well on the high ground about 300 yards from us, and were picking off some of our men.

The enemy was gaining strength and we were losing, so about 8:30 the Officer in Command decided to withdraw to safer ground a couple of miles away. The wounded that could walk would go with them... the others must be left behind. The Medical Aid men drew straws to see which one remained with the wounded. A boy named Fisher drew the short straw. I told the Regimental Surgeon that I was staying with the wounded. The Germans had perpetrated so many atrocities that I thought I might be able to keep the men from getting panicky and possibly keep the Germans from adding another crime to their list. As soon as the last of our forces had left I made a white flag from a sheet and hung it out the door. One boy had just had a hand grenade go off in his pocket and the doctor, before he left, told me that only a miracle could save the boy's life. I gave the lad two blood plasma units at once and spent all night running between the seriously wounded patients and the white flag. Every fifteen minutes I would go out and wave the white flag, because I was afraid the Germans, suspecting a trap, would fire hand grenades and mortars into the house before approaching it.

All night long this went on. The boy with the grenade wound died about four a. m. in my arms... a peaceful and holy death clutching the crucifix which I had taken down from the wall. All the boys joined in prayers for him. The Medic and myself changed all the bandages of the men, and as I was cooking some hot chocolate I looked out and saw Germans set up a machine-gun in the front yard. I grabbed the white flag and went out. A German jumped at me and stuck a gun in my stomach.

Well, a couple of paratroopers (German) marched me up the road about a quarter of a mile. One of them pushed me against a hedgerow and the two stepped back about ten feet and pulled back the bolts of their weapons. I said a quick Act of Contrition. (Upon later reflection and experience I discovered that whenever I was in any great danger, and was scared, instead of the Act of Contrition which I intended and tried to say, I always said the grace before meals.) Just then there were some shots fired just a few feet over our heads. It was a German noncom firing to attract the attention of the men I was with. He came running down the road and stopped when he reached us. He was a fine looking tough soldier about twenty-five. He spoke to my two captors and told me in broken English to come with him. I told him I was a Catholic priest and showed him my credentials. And to my real amazement he snapped to attention, saluted, made a slight bow, and showed me a medal pinned inside his uniform. (A great many German soldiers wear medals, badges, and carry prayer books.) He took me a little farther down the road to a German officer, who in turn called an Intelligence man. I explained that I was a Chaplain, knew nothing of military value and requested to be allowed to stay with my wounded men. The officer permitted this and my noncom friend took me back. The German paratroopers had ransacked the house of the little food we had, and picked up all the hand grenades that our men had left. The non-com, in a very friendly way, told me to stay with my "comrades" and that a German doctor would come in a day or so. I had to show him the wounds of all the men and practically every square inch of the house, i.e., drawers, cupboards, attic, etc. Then he left. But the paratroopers (German) dug in about the grounds and in the adjoining fields.

The wounded men had been frightened almost to death. One German had put a gun to one of the boys' head and pulled back the bolt; all the others turned their heads away. Another had shot the ceiling full of holes. The men were weak from fear and I told them that I had been too, but they were all quite calm. I spent the next few hours changing bandages and giving plasma, and fixed a bit of chocolate and what few rations we could scare up. The Germans were constantly running around outside the house, and apparently were planning to stay permanently.

The men gradually fell asleep and about ten p. m. I did so too. Just about midnight heavy shells began to fall and were landing on every side of us. One of the boys said it must be our own artillery trying to root the Germans out of this strategic high ground. The whole house bounced and shook for four hours. I put three of the men under the beds; the plaster was dropping all over the place, and the window glass had sprayed all over the room. Fourteen of the men were in one room, most of them very seriously wounded. Two men with sprained ankles were in the kitchen, and a Medic was in the barn holding down a boy who had gone out of his head, and who was trying to run out to the Germans. About 2:30 a. m. three shells made a direct hit on the house all at once. Half of the house completely collapsed on the two boys in the kitchen. I heard one of them call out "Father Sampson," and just as I got to the door the rest of the ceiling came down on the boy. I held his head in my arm and cleared away debris till I could touch his back. I felt his heart pump very hard for about one minute and then stop. I dug in the debris until I could touch the other boy. He was crushed beyond help and was dead. The roof of the kitchen and the entire wall was blown out (and the wall was almost two feet of stone thick).

I had the boys take turns in leading the others in the Lord's Prayer. Of all times and places for a religious argument! When one of the boys finished with "… for Thine is the Kingdom, and the Power, and the glory forever and ever," one of the Catholic men said that it didn't belong there. The Protestant men insisted that it did. The other Catholic men joined in to insist it didn't belong. I told them each say it in whichever way he had learned it. Scared as I was, this argument struck me so funny at the time that I almost became hysterical. Praying together seemed to calm the men, however. A flashlight had been blown out of the house and somehow turned on. It flooded the remainder of the house in light and was sure to draw fire both from our artillery and from the enemy, so I went out to turn it off. Just as I stepped out a German soldier brushed past me running for all he was worth, and as I reached to turn out the flashlight I saw another German in the creek about five feet away. He moved a bit, and when I lifted him up he died. I gave a quick absolution, and when I turned around to go back into the house I saw a German kneeling on one knee and leaning against the house. He had a machine gun across one knee pointing straight at me. I said what was supposed to be an Act of Contrition (grace before meals again, though, I am afraid) and ran into the house. The next morning when I came out the German was still there, in the same position. He was dead.

How we ever survived that night I shall never know, except that the calm fervent prayers of those wounded boys didn't leave God any choice in the matter but to answer them. After the artillery was through our infantry (501st) came up to close in. The house was riddled with rifle and machine gun fire. A tracer bullet ricocheted off the ceiling, grazed my leg and set my pants on fire. I saw an American lieutenant sneaking upon our building with hand grenades. It turned out to be Lieutenant Blackmon, an All American end for Alabama, who had taken over command of company B after Captain Bogart was killed. I ran out and stopped him, yelling for all I was worth. He said that he thought there were Germans in there. The Germans who were not killed were captured. Ours was the only room left standing in the entire village. Blackmon told me that the body of "Hap" Houlihan, of Ventura, California, one of the finest, most wholesome, and most devout lads in the Regiment, was lying on the road a few yards down the hill. This boy was a favorite of mine. He was the personification of all those fine qualities of heart and mind that we associate with an idealized "typical American boy."

In a great hurry, we evacuated the wounded men to the Division Hospital. The hospital was set up in an enormous French chateau. There was a wall around the chateau and the other buildings that made it look like a fortress. There were between two and three hundred wounded lying on the lawn, and about the same number in the chateau.

The hospital Chaplain, Fr. Durren, looked completely washed out. He had had scarcely any sleep either since the hospital had set up. I told him to go to bed, and that I would take over. He did so, but made me promise to wake him at two a. m. It was then seven p. m. Father had tagged the men he had anointed, and marked the men whose confessions he had heard. They were coming in steadily, however, wounded Americans and Germans. I had picked up enough German to ask if they were Catholic and to tell them that I was a priest. About sixty per cent of them were Catholic, and they always made the Sign of the Cross when I took out the stole. They made Acts of Contrition and received Viaticum reverently as well-instructed and good Catholics. These, I later learned, were mostly from Bavaria. Many of them were in their early teens; some had not begun to shave.

A touching incident occurred as I was going from one to another hearing confessions and anointing; and for the Protestant and Jewish boys saying a prayer with them and helping them to make an Act of Contrition. I had anointed a German boy who was horribly wounded — his abdomen had been ripped open and his intestines and other organs had bulged out and hung down. An American boy with a serious head wound lay on a stretcher about twelve feet away. The Medic had tucked a folded blanket under the head of the American, but the blanket had slipped off his litter, and he was groaning because of the painful position of his head. The German soldier crawled off his litter and along the floor on his back to the side of the American, fixed the folded blanket under his head again, and crawled back to his own litter. The German boy died within the hour.

I remained at the hospital until noon the following day, sleeping from three until six a. m. I did not wake up Fr. Durren until seven a. m., as he had been completely exhausted. Front line duty is not nearly as tiring as hospital duty, especially when the wounded keep pouring in as they did those first few days. A lieutenant of my outfit arrived with a couple of wounded boys and told me that the Regiment was assembling at a nearby town. He drove me there in his jeep. I reported in, and went to find a place to sleep, for I could scarcely move by this time. A couple of boys from our demolition section dug a deep comfortable foxhole for me and bedded it down with a parachute. Just as I was about to lie down, a German medium bomber, coming over at about twelve hundred feet, shut off his motors and dropped three small bombs. The Regimental staff came running out of the buildings at the approach of the plane, and didn't stop for permission to use any foxholes. It gave the boys quite a laugh to see the brass taking running dives for the nearest holes. The bombs landed right in the middle of the field we were in, but the only casualties were three cows. If the whole German Luftwaffe came over, it couldn't have kept me from going to sleep. I slept twenty-four hours straight through.

Thursday, after a full day's sleep, I went to Headquarters to see how well we had accomplished our mission, and found that we had done a one hundred per cent job. We had done so well, in fact, that another mission was to be added. However, only 950 men could be accounted for out of our jumping list of 2100. A couple of hundred men later dribbled in, in small groups.

One of our men told me that the mayor of the town would like to see me. He took me to him. The mayor's twelve-year-old son had been killed in the fighting in the town a couple of days before. Two Germans had used the boy as a shield, each holding one of his arms as they crossed the road. American machine gun fire killed all three. The mayor was bitter only against the Germans. The local priest was in a concentration camp (for listening to a radio which he had not given up as was required by the Germans), and the mayor wanted me to hold the funeral for the boy. I held the funeral the following morning, and a large number of my own men attended. The family could not express their gratitude enough. They invited me to dinner the following Sunday.

Friday evening the Germans bombed the Division Hospital, and did a very thorough job of it with just two giant bombs, probably three thousand pounders. The bombing was probably accidental. One bomb hit the corner of the chateau, and the other about fifty yards away. Fortunately, practically all the patients had been evacuated that afternoon. The seven patients that remained were killed. Six medical aid men, one doctor, and five prisoners were also killed. Fr. Durren fortunately escaped serious injury. The bomb that landed in the field by the hospital dug a tremendous crater, forty-two feet deep and eighty-five feet across. Two boys were sleeping in a foxhole right beside it and were not injured although they were entirely covered with earth after being tossed up in the air several feet by the concussion.

Saturday morning I went to the place where the Divisional cemetery had been established. None of the bodies had been buried yet, but there were several hundred lying side by side, waiting to be buried, each one in a parachute. I was shocked to find so many of my faithful boys among the dead. It didn't seem possible that these young men who had been so confident a week before, and whose hands I had shaken before we boarded the planes, and who had joked and wise-cracked that "no Hienie bullet has my name on it"… that they were in eternity now… O'Callahan from Indianapolis, Neumann from Minneapolis, Houlihan from Ventura, Roberts from Detroit, Rodriguez from El Paso, McMahon from Jacksonville, etc… they seemed like younger brothers… all in God's merciful hands now. German prisoners were digging the graves for both the American and the German dead. I read the burial ritual for all, and remained most of the afternoon for the actual burial.

Sunday I had Mass for the Regiment in the village church of Vierville. The church was quite small, a quaint old Norman building several hundred years old. A few civilians had come early, and the Americans packed the place, filling the sanctuary, the choir loft, and even crowding up on the altar steps. I am sure that no Catholic missed Mass on that day. We all felt that we had escaped death only through God's providential care. That afternoon with Sergeant Bordeleau, who spoke fluent French, I had dinner at the mayor's home. The head of the French underground for that area was a guest as well. He and the mayor explained to us how the underground worked. Every German collaborator in his district, he said, had been tagged and would be taken care of.

Sunday evening I attached myself to our 2nd Bn., which moved out toward Carentan to attack the German positions on the high ground just south of the city. We started the attack at dawn. We had to cross a stream and an open swamp that made our men easy targets for Jerry snipers and mortar fire. Our casualties were extreme the first hour, mostly wounded, however. I kept very busy working with the aid men hauling wounded out of the swamp. Somehow or other I felt sure that I would not be hit, and this was one of those rare occasions when I was not particularly afraid; I was too busy to think about it.

The next day German snipers and German artillery made it hot for us. Having taken the heights south of Carentan we started to dig in to hold the ground. The 88's zeroed in on us and for an hour and a half we were under the heaviest barrage the Regiment had seen so far. German tanks had flanked us and we were in danger of being cut off. I worked during this time with a litter crew going after the wounded, and the demands from all the companies for litters and help were more than we could supply — it was a terrific time. Men would come out of their fox holes when they saw me, to go to confession.

I had run into the abandoned aid station to pick up some sulfa-nilimide when an 88 hit the house and caved in the kitchen, showering me with plaster and debris in the next room, and I temporarily lost my sense of hearing. I was stone deaf for about forty minutes, and then my hearing gradually came back to normal.

In combat even close calls get monotonous, and one gets careless and reckless. But just when you get to thinking that you can take care of yourself in any emergency, something happens to remind you that you are still mortal. Strange thing, morale was the highest when the going was toughest. In the thick of things there seems actually to be a zest for battle that makes it as interesting as a big traditional football game. When it is over, it is a disgusting thing to realize how eager you were to play in this rotten kind of game. Only occasionally would I feel any emotion at the sight of a body, although I always stopped to say a prayer for the soldier whether American or German. Once in a while the sight of a boy I knew especially well would choke me up — his expression in death did not resemble his normal happy-go-lucky manner.

Confession and Communion are the greatest comfort to our men at the front, and non-Catholics have observed with open envy our Catholics receiving the sacraments. Many non-Catholic boys have come to confession at the front, and not infrequently I have discovered that they received Communion from me without my realizing who they were. I heard confessions and celebrated Mass under every conceivable circumstance. One Sunday the CO told me that he thought it would be safe to hold Mass in the reserve Bn. under a grove of trees. A large number gathered there, and I started to say Mass, using my jeep as an altar. Some German artillery observer must have spotted us. 88's began to fall all around us, and at the elevation a shell threw debris all over the jeep and altar. I turned around and told the men to hit their holes, which they did — but quick. I finished Mass in two minutes flat — record time.

One afternoon Captain Rhett, commander of headquarters company 2d Bn., and I were sitting on a mound paralleling a hedgerow just discussing the general situation. We were out of range of small-arms fire, or so we thought. Two bullets whistled past our heads; there was no mistaking the intention behind them. Captain Rhett had dug a foxhole a few feet away. We both took a dive for it... but I got there first. The captain tried to edge in, but there just wasn't room. Two more bullets kicked up little sprays of dirt a couple feet away. Rhett lay flat on his stomach using language very unbecoming an officer and a gentleman, nor did he take kindly to my censure.

A little later in the day Rhett saw a chance to get even. He asked me in the presence of his men if I would like to go on a little patrol with him. He knew perfectly well that I did not, but I didn't want to say so with men there... they'd have thought I was "chicken." "Why sure," I said, "I'd be glad to go along." We had not gone far when the platoon was fired on from two sides. We hit the ditches, myself right behind the captain. The enemy were few, but their fire was rather heavy. Someone up front called for a Medic. A man was wounded.

"That's you, Chaplain, you're the only one here with an aid kit," the captain said over his shoulder as he lay flat on the ground trying to size up the situation. Normandy is cattle country, and as I ran past Rhett I stepped in something always found in cattle country. My foot slipped and the captain took it full in the face. The man that had called for a Medic had only a flesh wound in the shoulder. Corporal Hoff, who spoke German, called out to the German patrol that were opposing us to surrender, for we had them in a tight spot. Three of them came in with their hands above their heads. Two Germans were dead, one was dying. Three or four others got away. As we went back, Captain Rhett glared at me and swore that he would never go to church again, a promise he has happily failed to keep.

After three weeks in combat we were told that we were going to Cherbourg to garrison the vicinity of that city for a couple of weeks. On the way up there we stopped at Sainte Mere Eglise where all those who had died in the invasion had been moved to and reburied in three tremendous cemeteries. I said two Requiem Masses there — one for my men and one for Fr. Maternowski, O.F.M. Conv., the Chaplain for the 5O8th Parachute Inf. Reg., who was killed on D Day while he was helping a group of men out of a glider that was under machine gun fire. Fr. Maternowski was a great priest, a tough and energetic little Pole, who had been extremely well liked by the men of his Regiment. On more than one occasion he had volunteered to put the gloves on with officers who interfered with his work or who tried to wise-crack about the Church or made smart remarks about confession. To the best of my knowledge no one ever took him up on the invitation, but even those with whom he had difficulties respected him.

His method of straightening things out was very effective, even though unconventional. His boys would never forget Fr. Maternowski, and would thereafter be better men for having known a priest who had deliberately given his life for his men.

The French people of the little city of Sainte Mere Eglise had arranged that each family adopt a couple of graves. On Sundays and Holy Days they bedecked them with flowers, and they promised to remember always these soldiers in their prayers.

On the way to Cherbourg we passed through a town where the Free French were having a riotous time shaving the heads and stripping the women collaborators and marching them through the streets. A French priest who had spent considerable time in a German concentration camp told me that the very ones who cut the hair and ripped off the women's clothing had themselves been very friendly and helpful to the Germans. In Paris and other large French cities, our forces were cheered and wined and dined by the "patriotic" populace. But our boys who had been captured by the Germans and marched through to prison camps a couple of months before had been spat upon, kicked, and hooted at by the people of these same cities.

The Regiment was stationed a couple miles from the city and just outside the walls of a tremendous convent — a mother house, school, novitiate, and hospital of some French order. About twelve of the fourteen buildings had been completely flattened by our bombers — the Germans had been using it. About fifty sisters were still there, and not one of them had been scratched by the bombing. They had been in the deep cellar of the twelfth century main building that was burned to the ground... the eight hundred-year-old basement had four-foot walls that held firm. I asked the sisters for permission to use what remained of their hospital for our sick and some recently wounded. They were happy to allow us, and were as solicitous as they could be — the most wonderful group of women that I have ever known. Their convent had been burned down some twenty years before, rebuilt, and now they were stacking the still warm bricks in piles and getting ready to build again. Their magnificent chapel had been caved in on two sides, the roof now piled up on the floor, but the good sisters were clearing away the debris as best they could.

The marvelous (maybe I should say "miraculous") thing about this chapel is the life-sized crucifix hanging above the side altar... It was not even scratched, and although I studied the altar below it and the ceiling that had crashed down I could not find any possible explanation for the crucifix escaping serious damage, for it hung at least three feet from the wall. Splendid life-sized statues of Sts. Peter and Paul stood unharmed in niches on each side of the crucifix. I may be credulous, but to me that was a miracle of providential protection, and so the nuns looked upon it. I asked for permission to say Mass there, and the nuns were delighted. I sent a runner to assemble the Catholics of the Regiment. — Many Protestants also attended. The sisters cleared the debris from the altar, but the tabernacle was smashed, and bricks, plaster and beams under foot made it difficult to move about. I shall never forget that Mass as long as I live.

I spoke to the men something like this. "The image of the naked Galilean hanging from the cross has always inspired great love and fierce hate. Nero sought to make the cross a hateful image by putting Christians to death on it, pouring pitch upon them and lighting Rome with these flaming human crosses. Julian the Apostate said that he would make the world forget the Man on the cross, but in his final agony had to acknowledge: 'Thou has conquered, Galilean.' Henry VIII for an extra wife was willing to strip the cross of Christ's body, and some foolish people have become puritanically ashamed of the image of their salvation. Communists forbid its presence because they fear its power against their evil designs. Hitler has tried to replace the image of our Blessed Lord on the cross with a stupid swastika. Invectives, false philosophies, violence, and every diabolical scheme has been used to tear the Christ from the cross, and the crucifix from the church. But, like the bombs that were dropped on this chapel, they have only succeeded in making the cross stand out more and more in bold relief, and the image we love grows greater in our understanding, because of the vehemence of the hate it occasions in wicked men. Each of us has that sacred image stamped upon his soul. Like this chapel, we are temples of God. And no matter how the shells of temptation may assail us, no matter how we are torn by the bombs of tragedy and trial and assault from without, the image of the Crucified remains… if we want it to. Now, at the foot of this cross, let us renew our baptismal vows, and let us promise to shield forever His image in our hearts."

We left the convent the following day. The sisters gave literally hundreds of rosaries and medals to my men. A windfall gave me the opportunity of repaying the sisters for their kindness. Our supply officer told me that he had dozens of every type of brush and broom, lime, piles and piles of soap, and many other such things that we had no further use for, and this gift to the sisters was received with such expressions of gratitude that I was embarrassed.

At Cherbourg we remained for about two weeks. We were stationed about three miles from the city. I held my Masses in a beautiful little French church in a village nearby. The French people were always very much impressed by the large number of American men attending Mass and especially the sacraments. Every French priest commented upon it with wonder and admiration. This particular church had been hit several times by 88 shells but was far from ruined. The pastor's home, however, was in complete ruin. I took up a collection each Sunday for him from our men. Seven thousand francs was donated one Sunday and eight thousand the following Sunday. The poor priest, with tears in his eyes, tried desperately to tell me how grateful he was… and that this was more than his congregation had been able to contribute in a whole year. I have never met a French priest who did not impress me as being a really spiritual man.

When the Regiment was bivouacked near Utah beach waiting for the boats to take us back to England, a young soldier by the name of Fritz Nyland came to see me. He was very troubled in mind. The company commander of his brother, who was with the 508 Parachute Regiment, told Fritz that this brother had been killed, and was buried in Sainte Mere Eglise cemetery. We jumped in my jeep and drove the twenty miles back to that town. In checking the cemetery roster I couldn't find the boy's name.

"There's no William Nyland listed here, Fritz," I said encouragingly, "though there is a Roland Nyland listed."

"Oh gosh, Father, that's my brother too. He was a lieutenant in the Ninetieth Division." The unhappy boy tried to choke back the tears. We said a few prayers at the grave, then went to another cemetery just a few blocks away where we found the grave we were looking for originally. A third brother had just been killed in the Pacific.

As we were driving back to the bivouac area Fritz kept saying over and over again, more to himself than to me, "What will poor Butch do now? What will poor Butch do now?"

"Who is Butch, son?" I asked.

"Butch? Oh, she's my mother." I looked at him and wondered if he was suffering from combat exhaustion and the terrible shock of this afternoon's discovery. He must have read my thoughts, for he explained, "We four boys always called mom 'Butch' these last few years. That's because, when we wanted to listen to swing orchestras and jive bands on the radio, mom would always turn it on to 'gangbusters' or to some program about gangsters. Now I'm the only one left." Mrs. Nyland had received three tragic wires within a week. However, we managed to get Fritz sent back to the states, so 'Butch' still has one son to comfort her.

I never thought that I would want to see England again, but it was almost like coming home. On the boat going back I spent nearly all my time cutting the men's hair. The rival GI barbers claimed it wasn't fair — they couldn't compete with my bargain of a haircut and confession both.

Now came the most difficult job of all — writing to all the parents or wives of the men we had lost in combat. I tried desperately to make each letter as personal as possible, and since in most cases I knew the men quite well, I could speak about the last time I saw them, and bring out some kindly trait that the family would recognize. However, this was only partially successful, and most of the letters sounded very much alike.

We were not in England long before we were preparing for another mission. About this time I began to receive answers from the parents and wives of our deceased boys. They were among the greatest consolations I have received as a priest, I shall always cherish them. It was marvelous to see with what courage and fortitude and faith these people accepted the terrible sacrifice that was demanded of them.

CHAPTER V: THE JUMP INTO HOLLAND

The old tent city outside of Newbury looked pretty good to us, and the band was out to give us a rousing welcome. Seven-day furloughs were granted and the men took off for London to tear the city apart, although they were given some stiff competition in this respect by the buzz bombs. The buzz bombs had started coming over England the day of the invasion, and the effect on the British was even more staggering than the blitz had been during the first couple years of the war. There were no raid warnings for the buzz zombs, and it was impossible to take adequate shelter for they kept coming over all day and night. One of these bombs lit in the middle of the street killing thirty-two Americans riding in a bus.

The Franciscan sisters at Coldash had all the chaplains of the area up for a special home-coming dinner. As always the dinner was grand, but the real surprise came during the middle of the meal. Dozens of silver airplanes covered the ceiling of the dining room. Silk threads that you couldn't see were pulled by someone in the next room opening the bomb-bay doors of the planes, and dozens of little men with paper parachutes floated down, each with a large "Welcome home" sign on his chest.

The children wanted to know what happened to this man and that man; each asked about the men she had prayed for. One little freckled-faced red-headed tyke with a tooth out in front tugged at my trousers and asked if "Happy" Houlihan was all right. I swallowed hard and told her that "Hap" was dead. I could have bawled when her lovable little face drooped and tears began to well in her eyes. But then she perked right up again. "Oh, then he is with Jesus." Everything was all right. Do you blame me for picking her up and almost hugging the life out of her?

I spent two days of my furlough in London relaxing at the Regent Hotel whenever the buzz bombs would grant a couple hours respite. I saw the Lunts in a Robert Sherwood play, someone else in "Arsenic and Old Lace," and Bing Crosby and Barry Fitzgerald in "Going My Way." I returned to Newbury and a four-day retreat at the monastery. The Fathers were most kind, and the peace and quiet of those days was just what I needed.

We were alerted again the first of September, and were all ready to board the planes to jump behind the German lines at Le Mans, France, when word came down that the jump was cancelled. Patton's men were covering ground faster than they could plan another Airborne operation. At a Division review General Eisenhower thanked the men for what they had done in Normandy, decorated those who had distinguished themselves in a special manner, and stated that he looked to the 101st to justify his great confidence in future operations. In other words, our combat had really just begun. Everyone swallowed hard on that one.

The battalion that had been stationed at Lambourne was at this time moved over to the regimental area, and consequently more tents had to be put up, mess halls built and so forth. As this was going on one day the Countess Craven, on whose estate we were located, made a tour of the grounds, accompanied by the keeper of the hounds and several of her dogs. She paused near a lieutenant and myself. The lieutenant, a slow-drawling young giant from Texas, more to make conversation and to be pleasant than anything else, spoke to the Countess, "Lots of construction going on, isn't there, ma'am?"

"Construction! Don't be impertinent, young man," she said scornfully and with a tone of bitterness. "Destruction, don't you mean?" pointing with her cane to the building the lieutenant was supervising.

"Well, ma'm," said the Texan, his face getting very red, "I guess you'll have to ask the boys who died to save your damn estate the answer to that question." He started to walk away, then turned to me. "I'm sorry, Father, but I'm sore… damn sore."

September 16 we were briefed for our mission in Holland. I managed to get all the Catholics together for Mass, and everyone received Holy Communion. As before the jump in France, I again shook hands with the men as they left the hangars to go to their respective planes; a large number of the men knelt for a blessing. We took off at eleven a. m., flew over the Channel, escorted by P-47s; over Brittany and northern France; over Belgium, which was beautiful from the air; and then into Holland. There was not nearly as much flak sent up at us as in France. At ten minutes of one we stood up and hooked up. It was a beautiful day. At 1:10 we jumped. As soon as I left the door I saw a large castle below with a wide moat encircling it. My chute opened well, but I had scarcely got my bearings again when I saw that I was swinging onto the top of another man's chute. I landed almost in the middle of his chute and sank as if in quicksand. I lay down and tried to roll off. In the meantime my own chute collapsed and hung down. I rolled off his chute and my own blossomed out again and just in time — I was less than 100 feet from the ground, or I should say from the water. I think that was the closest that I ever came to death by jumping. I lit squarely in the middle of the moat but fortunately the water was only up to my chest. Since I was not nearly as heavily loaded down as in France, I was able to make the edge, and to climb up and over the fence about it. I had not heard a shot fired, and the day was so beautiful that it seemed like a parade ground jump. That illusion was dispelled a couple of hours later.

The man on whose chute I had fallen had landed in deeper water. I was able to get hold of his chute and to drag him in, before I got out of the moat. Quite a few men had landed in trees, and there were many with broken arms and legs, and back injuries. I located Dr. Kingston who had jumped in my plane. He had landed in a tree and had hurt his back getting out. A drawbridge from the castle was over the moat, and the doctor suggested that we set up an aid station there immediately. Several Medics were about and began bringing the injured to the castle, which was now, we discovered, a museum with torture racks, implements for mutilation, scourges, iron masks, and fearful pictures of these things in operation hung all about the many rooms. Not the most ideal setting to inspire confidence in an army doctor. The first patient had a broken arm and dislocated wrist. I held the arm while a Medic administered ether and the Doc pulled the bones in place. It didn't take more than three minutes. The boy woke up immediately with, "Gee, Father, are we home already?" Then, looking about him, he began to realize where he was and said, "Gosh, I had a swell dream about going home. How many hours have I been here?"

Doc Kingston asked me to try and contact Col. Kinnard, get our location, and find out if the aid station should stay where it was. A little Dutch town was only about a mile away and I went there looking for Col. Kinnard. The people were all out in the streets waving to the Americans, cheering, and offering cool fresh milk to Yanks. One of the soldiers told them that I was a priest, and you can't imagine the excitement; southern Holland is solidly Catholic and what Catholics! They went immediately and got the pastor, who literally pushed me up to the rectory, sat me down to a big meal, and summoned the village barber (for I had a beard... we always wear them into combat — makes you look tough). First, however, I got hold of a couple of GIs and told them to locate Col. Kinnard and come back and let me know where he was. Then I had the fine dinner, was shaved, and went outside, where a whole monastery of Norbertines were waiting to greet me. I had to shake everyone's hand. They all spoke English and all at once. This didn't seem much like real combat, or if it was I could take a lot more of the same kind of combat.

The two GIs came back. They had located Col. Kinnard and I went to him to get the dope. He told me that we were nearly eight miles off our DZ and that Bn. would have to hurry up and get there before nightfall and take our objectives. He asked me to tell the Doc, get transportation for the patients if possible, and follow. I hurried back to the castle, told Kingston, and he asked me to get some vehicles if I could. I went back into town, but there was not a serviceable truck there. I then went back toward the castle, and when I got to within 300 yards of the place I saw Germans all around. There were a few shots, but they had taken the place without any opposition. Capt. Byrd, who had been left there to form a road block with a few GIs had been killed, I learned later, with three of his men. I was lucky not to have been seen, so I hightailed it back to town, got a scooter-bike and set out after Col. Kinnard, whom I located in Veghel, our original objective. I gave him the story, and he sent a platoon to try and retake the Medics and wounded, but it was too late. They had been evacuated by the Germans.

Then things began to pop from all quarters. Our holiday jump turned into a nightmare for the next few hours. Then the Germans withdrew, but we knew that it was only to try to encircle us, and that in a couple of days we would really be in for it. Our Regimental Aid Station was set up in the magnificent and up-to-the-minute hospital of the town of Veghel, and operated by a splendid Dutch order of nuns. The priest chaplain of the hospital was very gracious — got out all his pre-war tobacco, and the radio which he had hid for four years. I couldn't convince him that a real battle was still to be fought. Our casualties were very small so far; the German artillery had not hurt us as badly as it had the civilians. The two Dutch doctors at the hospital were very good and we became good friends. The younger doctor, Leo, became one of the finest friends I had made since I left the States. Our Regimental surgeon later told me that Leo was one of the most skillful and talented young doctors he had ever seen. In several cases he injected a stimulant directly to the heart with a needle to pull a man out of severe shock, and saved lives with his fearless surgery.

The British armored column was long overdue. They were to push through in eighteen hours, and we did not even see them until the fourth day, when they stopped at four p. m., made their tea, and prepared to bed down for the night. No wonder their own paratroopers at Arnheim were cut to ribbons. To get ahead of the story a little bit, some time later, at a dinner party of American officers, an English tank officer was present. The Englishman was bragging about the efficiency of British armored units. One of our men couldn't stand it any longer. In a slow southern drawl he proceeded to tell the Britisher off. "Efficient? An American Boy Scout with a screwdriver, lying in a hole in the ground, could take your tanks apart one by one as they go into battle!"

One day I was walking along the tracks at the edge of Veghel when I saw a platoon coming up a dirt road through the woods. I sat down and waited for them, thinking that I would attach myself to them for the day. When they were about 200 yards away I raised my field glasses and took a look. They were Germans. I took a nose-dive for the other side of the tracks and heard a couple of shots whine uncomfortably close overhead. The really strange part of paratroop operations is the constant presence on all sides of you of the enemy, and of the infiltration of each side into the other "lines." I hurried to tell the nearest unit commander about the German platoon — a glider Reg. Hq. was only a couple of blocks away. They immediately put a platoon on the job.

We were in the vicinity of Veghel about two weeks. The town was heavily shelled by the Germans, and a large number of civilians were killed and several sisters of the hospital too. The patients were taken to the basement of the hospital, and when I visited it they were all saying the rosary in unison. Veghel was as beautiful a little city as I have ever seen. Its church was really magnificent. It is impossible to describe how clean the Dutch are. Their homes are regular doll houses and very, very modern, far ahead of England or any place else that I have seen in Europe, and I would even say that the standard of living seemed to me to be above that of the United States. Cleanliness was a fetish. They scrubbed their sidewalks, and I would not have hesitated to eat off the brick street in front of the church.

I attached myself to the 1st Bn. when it set out to take a key town about ten miles away. It was to be a surprise move and we arrived at the town about one a. m. But we did not surprise the Dutch underground, which was the best in all Europe. A Dutch priest was waiting for us; the Bn. staff went to his house, and he told us that he had some ninety men armed ready to help us. He told us where every German guard position was, the number of Germans in the vicinity, and exactly where they were. As a result of this information, we took the town without the loss of a single American life, and very few wounded. About sixty Germans were killed, a couple hundred wounded, and over 500 taken prisoner, and our own Bn. strength had been only about 400. We had to leave there in a hurry, however, and get our prisoners back to Div. PW, for German tanks were coming toward town and we had nothing to cope with tanks. I felt badly for the townspeople, who hated to see us leave; they had been so happy at their liberation. They welcomed us into their homes for a grand meal before we left. When the tanks did get into town, we were a couple of miles beyond and had set up road and tank blocks. Then we watched British typhoons with rockets go to work on the tanks. A plane peeling off at you with those terrifying screaming rockets is something that is not pleasant to contemplate.

We spent another week about Veghel and the fighting became intense. In a Regiment of 2000 men spread over a considerable area it is difficult for a chaplain to be present at the right places at the right times when his men need him most. But Providence certainly guided my steps more than ever during these days, for scarcely a single Catholic died during this time without my being present to administer the last rites. I was carrying the Blessed Sacrament with me wherever I went. I stopped in at a farm house being used as battalion CP, and a young soldier by the name of Maloney, a battalion runner, wanted to go to confession and receive Holy Communion. When we had taken care of this the CO gave him a message to take to one of the companies. Just as he was about to leave a stray bullet came through the door and went right through the boy's heart. His Communion of a few minutes before had become his Viaticum. Just then a soldier came in and said that a tree burst had hit one of the men a couple hundred yards away. When I got there I found that it was the regiment's other Maloney. He was dying. Extreme Unction and Viaticum fortified him for a very holy death. It was uncanny the way God was providing His greatest gifts and helps at life's crucial moment for His boys, through the medium of a very bewildered, scared, and unworthy priest.

We now moved up to Nijmegen; I rode a scooter-bike up there, since my jeep had not yet come in. On the way up I stopped off at Uden to see the famous church there. The town was only 9000 and the church was as large as St. Patrick's in New York, and, I thought, more beautiful. I stopped in at a Crozier monastery for dinner, and, believe it or not, one of the first priests I met was a fellow I had known as a seminarian at Catholic U., in Washington, D.C. The monastery had been used as a German officers training school, and the monks were really happy to see an American priest. They had all sorts of questions to ask about their missions in Minnesota and their school in Onamia.

The first couple of days fighting was really terrific, and the casualties heavy. We began to realize that we were going to lose more men in this operation than we did in France. Our Regiment clashed with a German regiment at the dyke, and it became a battle of pitching grenades over the dyke at each other. The Germans, under cover of fog at night, finally pulled back across the Rhine.

It was at this time that Col. Johnson, our Reg. CO, was killed by a mortar shell. He lived for an hour or more after he was hit. In France he had attended the Mass I spoke about earlier in this narrative. He had called me in that night, and told me that he had been thinking about coming into the Catholic Church. As he put it "It is the only Church with enough guts to demand obedience and sacrifice [soldier virtues that he could understand] and the only one capable of understanding and dealing mercifully with weak human nature." I thought that he hit the nail right on the head, but didn't want him to think that he was doing the Church a great favor by coming in. So I told him all the obligations that would be his as a Catholic. He was a man of tireless energy, unlimited ambition, and boundless enthusiasm, with lots of color and a great personality. I sincerely regret not having been with him before he died, for I am sure I could have baptized him into the Church.

Lieutenant Colonel Julian J. Ewell took over the regiment, and he will always stand out in my mind as the perfect example of the officer and the gentleman… West Pointer of '39 class. Whenever a Company was going to be given a particularly difficult and dangerous mission he would notify Chaplain Engel and myself, so that we could hold our respective services. He had the keenest droll wit that I have ever known. During his first week as CO pressure was brought to bear from higher up because of looting, and because too many cows were ending up in GI frying pans (they didn't know the password). The Dutch had complained to the army authorities. Ewell was inspecting one of the battalions, and it seemed that all the men were eating big two-inch steaks and pork chops; hams were hanging up in the trees, and chicken feathers all over the place gave evidence of a real variety in the menu. But the battalion CO was a resourceful fellow and had an excuse for everything. The cattle had been hit by 88s, the pigs had stepped on mines, the chickens had just died — from battle fatigue presumably. "Better to eat the things than to let them go to waste." Finally they came upon a couple of GIs chasing a pig and shooting at it. The regimental CO turned to the battalion CO and said dryly, "Look! I suppose you're going to tell me now that that pig is attacking your men."

It was at this time that Notre Dame played Army and took the 59-0 shellacking. But that was nothing compared to the shellacking I took from the Regiment's West Pointers. They really turned the heat on.

On a Sunday I went up to the dyke to say Mass for the men on the MLR (main line of resistance). There was a nice little church beside the dyke, and the civilians, having been told by the GIs that there was to be Mass, came too in crowds. But the Germans started an intense barrage in that area. Of course, the battle-wise GIs took to their fox-holes, but the civilians, thinking that shells are only meant to kill soldiers, calmly filed along the top of the dyke and to church. Maybe it was their faith saved them and me. Why a number of this group were not killed by 88s landing all about them I don't know. After Mass I went to the Bn. headquarters, and the 88s really started to open up again.

Three shells landed every minute for about forty minutes, with about one out of five a dud. Something happened then to make real Christians out of several men. I was with the Bn. staff in a farmhouse which had received a direct hit on the empty room facing the German front. The barn was attached to the house, and had about twenty GIs in it. One fellow was lying on an old mattress next to the wall and had his legs spread apart. An 88 came through the roof, right between his legs and buried itself in the concrete floor. It was a dud. The boy was about paralyzed with fright and the perspiration just rolled off him. He had quite a reputation as an exaggerator, and when he got his speech back groaned, "Nobody will ever believe me when I tell them about this."

At night I would sometimes stay in a dugout with a couple of GIs, and the worse the weather the higher their morale, because it taxes their ingenuity to find ways of making themselves comfortable and keeping dry. It was quite a lesson in psychology.

One evening after Mass a couple of my best boys stopped to talk with me for a while. One of them had just received a box of holy cards from his sister, a nun, and he gave these to me to distribute among the men. The other was my regular server who had asked me to buy a crucifix when I was in town, for his mother. I gave him the crucifix and he told me how much his mother would appreciate it. As I was pulling out fifteen minutes later the place was hit by an 88 and the two boys were instantly killed. As I knelt to anoint them, war never seemed more horrible and useless than it did then. They had just received Holy Communion at Mass. I was choked up for the rest of the day.

Before we left Holland we were told that we would have a Regimental memorial ceremony at the cemetery. It is really shocking when you look upon row after row of white crosses, each one representing a young man you knew so well, so full of life before, so anxious to get home to his loved ones and they so anxious to see him again, now lying here in Holland. Chaplain Engle said a short appropriate prayer; the Colonel called out the names, spoke a few words of sincere appreciation for all they did; then I addressed the men assembled in formation in a complete square about the cemetery. Taps were blown, and then the echo of taps was sounded from a distance. The Colonel had had a wreath of flowers placed on each grave. After the ceremony he walked over to Col. Johnson's grave and picked up a carnation from it. When he saw that I had observed him, he walked over to me and said, "I guess I'm a little soft, Father, but I thought his wife might like to have it." He isn't half as cold-blooded a soldier as many think.

A couple of days later we pulled out, and were replaced by the British. The Holland operation was finished. We got out just in time, for that night the Germans dynamited the dykes and flooded that whole area.

CHAPTER VI: THE DEFENSE OF BASTOGNE

We drove back through Holland, Belgium, into France, and just beyond Rheims to Mourmelon where we were to be quartered in an old French infantry camp. The Germans had been garrisoned there, but had left in such a hurry that they had not ruined anything. As a matter of fact, they had made some very fine improvements in the place. I arrived on a Sunday, and since the rest of the Regiment had not yet arrived, Chaplain Engle suggested that we drive the eighteen miles back to Rheinis to see the cathedral, and I could say Mass there. The Rheims Cathedral is easily the most beautiful church I have ever seen. It is perfectly proportioned, lovely as a sonnet, and delicate as fine lace. Really, it is impossible to describe its ageless beauty. Although it has withstood the elements for 800 years, and though it was shelled badly in the last war, it remains yet a magnificent stone prayer. I have seen Notre Dame in Paris and it doesn't even approach Notre Dame of Rheims. I said Mass there on the Blessed Sacrament altar, and you can imagine how I felt about that. Chaplain Engle stayed for Mass. He is a great student of ecclesiastical architecture and especially of stained glass windows. I actually had to drag him away from the church after a couple of hours.

My office and room at Mourmelon were very nice and comfortable, and we prepared to settle down to training for the spring offensive next March (for we would never be used in the winter, we were told). We had lost too many men and the replacements would have to be thoroughly trained, new equipment procured, and many changes made in the Regiment. Yes, definitely, we would be here for at least five months. We were there three weeks (even less than that) when we were called up in the middle of the night to plug the gap of the great German break-through.

The Germans had built a beautiful big theatre on the post and so the five priests of the 101st Division decided that we would have High Mass there every Sunday. The theatre held 1500 and we packed it each Sunday. I had to organize and conduct the choir. We took turns in saying the Mass and in preaching, while the other priests heard confessions all during the Mass. It worked out well. I was quite proud of my choir, and we got down to serious work for the Christmas Mass. I had nearly ninety voices for that choir, and we had a trip scheduled to sing at several hospitals in and near Paris.

I was able to get to Paris a couple of times while stationed at Mourmelon, and even in war time that city is like no other in the world. It is the most beautiful city that I have ever seen, with an endless number of famous monuments and places of interest. Its morals are reminiscent of pagan Rome at its worst. I was fortunate enough to take in the ballet at the Paris Opera House, which place more than lived up to my expectations. The ballet was entertaining (my first), especially so when the ballerina, during one of her intricate twirls, fell kerplunk. She arose, however, smiled prettily, and carried it off quite well.

Chaplain Engle and I had just finished writing the letters to the families of our Holland casualties, when we were awakened at two a. m. on December 17th and told that the Germans were making a big break-through, and that we were to leave immediately to plug the gap. A large number of men were on pass, and the MPs in Paris, Rheims, Mourmelon and other cities were ordered to send all Airborne men back to their base camp immediately. These men would follow us up to Bastogne.

The whole regimental band came barging into my office as I was busy packing. They were mad. They had been ordered to stay behind again; they had joined the paratroopers because they wanted to fight in this war, they said. What did I think about their packing up and piling into the trucks going with us? I was on the spot, and evaded the question. But they must have guessed that I personally thought the CO would be mighty glad to have a few extra men to bolster our thinned-out companies. Each company in the regiment found a couple of band members in line with them at Bastogne, and they gave an excellent account of themselves. Several of them were wounded, though none of them killed.

We were leaving in such a hurry this time, and everyone was so busy throwing the few things together we were able to take with us, that there wasn't time to get the Regiment together for Mass, nor did I have time for confessions. I said a private Mass, and then just before we pulled out I went around to each company, called the Catholics together, gave general absolution and distributed Holy Communion. There were several hundred new men in the Regiment, replacements who had arrived only a week before and had had no battle experience as yet. These boys went into Bastogne inadequately equipped, but quickly absorbed the spirit of the regiment and did a splendid job.

Chaplain Engle and I threw our combat equipment into our barracks bags and bedrolls, piled them into my jeep

(Chaplain Engle didn't take his jeep), and away we went to Bastogne, about 150 miles away.

The first day was not too bad and our casualties not heavy. Reg. Hq. was, as usual, in a church building... a junior seminary. Many of the young boys were still there and the faculty. The second day I had a thriller that kept me sweating for an hour afterwards. Someone told me that there was a man between the lines who was wounded and they could hear him call for a priest. I asked the fellow to take me to him, and grabbed a Medic and we went up to find him. A German tank had been knocked out on the road between us and the wounded man, but a German was still manning the machine gun on the tank. As we started to climb through the fence he let go at us. The boy leading us had the upper bone in his arm shattered by a bullet. We all three took a dive to the ditch beside the railroad track. The wounded boy pointed out where the man I was looking for was and the Medic and myself went to him. We were pinned down to the bottom of the ditch by crossfire. I lay down beside the boy and heard his confession and anointed him. Not a word of complaint did he say. He said "Thanks" and that he felt everything was going to be all right now, and that he hoped nobody thought that he was yellow because he yelled for a priest. The Medic told me that he didn't have a chance, but we carried him back to the line, and some other men took him to the aid station. I never heard whether he lived or not — he was not out of our Regiment.

Combat exhaustion is a peculiar thing, and accounts for a large percentage of the casualties of a fighting outfit. Sometimes it would afflict men in very strange ways. One little fellow had given a wonderful account of himself in both Normandy and Holland; he was credited with knocking out a German tank with his bazooka, had volunteered for several very successful patrols, and had, on another occasion, helped wipe out a machine-gun nest. For these accomplishments he had been decorated twice. But the lad just couldn't stand artillery, and when the Germans were throwing in a few 88s at us he lay in his foxhole shaking like a leaf and crying. Day by day he got worse, and even our own shells going out frightened him. He protested being evacuated, but his hysterical fear of artillery had become a bad morale factor, for fear and hysteria are contagious. There was nothing wrong with this boy's courage; he had plenty of it — more than most men; but combat exhaustion had made him useless to the Regiment. There were numerous other cases in which men had been subject to as much fear and horror as they were capable of enduring, then broke under the pressure of further demands too great for them to sustain. These men were as sick and as serious casualties of battle as those wounded by bullets or by fragments of enemy shells, and their evacuation was just as honorable. But they were sometimes to suffer even further by the false accusations of their comrades, or by their own unfair suspicions regarding their courage.

On the 19th of December, I was sitting around after dinner with a group of service and Reg. Hq. Co. Men just shooting the breeze, when Mr. Sheen, the communication warrant officer came in. "you should see what I have just seen," he said, "a bunch of paratroopers machine gunned on this road." He didn't know whether they 501st men or not. I asked him where the place was, but he couldn't explain very well. I told the medical executive officer that I would be right back soon. My driver and I piled into the jeep and away we went. We couldn't find the bodies sheen had spoken about, so I decided to keep going a couple of miles farther on to where our division medical company had been captured by the Germans the night before. A few German vehicles, armored cars, etc., had come up from a side road, shot up several American trucks bringing in supplies, and captured our whole medical co. At the same time. Our own regimental supply trucks for the medics were captured there, and Doc Waldman had told me that we were getting very short of medical supplies. So I decided to salvage some of the stuff that the Germans left from our captured medical company. I loaded my jeep with a couple of chests of much-needed equipment, and was ready to head back for the Reg. Aid station. A soldier there told me, however, that there had been quite a skirmish last night on the other side of the hill. He thought there were still some wounded left there. We drove over the hill to see, and just over the crest of the hill we ran into Germans — hundreds of them. They jumped out from behind trees yelling something, and a couple of reconnaissance vehicles levelled their guns at us from about forty feet. I told the driver to stop, and that i was sorry to have gotten him into this mess. We were captured.

PART III: PRISON

CHAPTER VIII: THE JOURNEY TO STALAG II-A

A German lieutenant got into the car, and told me to keep driving down to the bottom of the hill, where there was a little town. The German soldiers there reminded me of a pack of rats. They had broken into a little warehouse, and they were dragging stuff out, and would smash canned goods on the cement to see if they wanted them or not. They had broken into the school and came out with musical instruments, and were blowing on them and beating the drums. The lieutenant started questioning me, but I told him my name, rank and serial number and said that that was all I could tell him. He seemed like a decent fellow and didn't press it any further. He went away for a bit, I presumed to call his CP about my capture. When he went the soldiers started after the stuff in my jeep. They threw out the medical equipment, Chaplain Engle's communion set which I tried to rescue but was prevented, our duffle bags, etc. I was glad that I had left my Mass kit in the aid station. Then they got the box of cookies my Aunt Millie had sent me for Christmas, and that really did go against the grain, for it had taken considerable self-control to save those cookies for Christmas.

Then, a mule faced boorish type German soldier grabbed my arm and yanked my wrist-watch off. I told him that I was a priest and an American captain and asked for it back, but he just laughed. A couple of soldiers began to argue with him, in my behalf I gathered, but without success. So I began yelling for a German officer as loudly as I could. The fellow started going away but I followed him still yelling. Finally, with what I took for German profanity, he handed my watch back. (That is lesson number 1 in dealing with German soldiers — yell at them, scream at them, get red in the face, distend your neck muscles, and be flushed with anger. Modesty and meekness never work. They will walk all over the humble man.) The lieutenant came back and assigned my driver and me to ride in a half-track which they had captured from the Americans.

The fifteen most miserable days I have ever spent on earth then began rather favorably. The three Germans in the half-track were young, and seemingly quite decent boys. We rode for five hours. One of the Germans could speak some English and told me all about his family. He and one of the other Germans were Catholic and all three very respectful. Since I couldn't be sure that they were not after information I let them do all the talking. They talked about everything, using the English-speaking boy as interpreter. I was amazed at their ignorance of the real issues of the war. On our way back to their rear we passed miles and miles of German armored vehicles and tanks and lots of our equipment which they had captured and were using. This was the line, I later discovered, which surrounded Bastogne, and demanded that the 101st surrender. Our General McAuliffe became famous with his "Nuts" reply. General McAuliffe is a Catholic and a very good one too.

At some little town in the middle of the night my driver and I were let out to join a group of other Americans who had been taken prisoner, and were marching to the rear. We stopped briefly to be interrogated by a German Intelligence Officer. Then we marched until two a. m., when we were herded into a filthy barn in a little town. We remained there that night and the following day, and despite my pounding on the door demanding water and food, we received none. I was the only officer in the group and consequently had to try to keep morale up and discipline, for lack of these things give the German interrogators the opening they want. About eleven p. m. the second night a German Intelligence Officer came out and called for me. He said that he hadn't known that there was an officer in the group (which I knew was a lie), and that I would have received better treatment. He started his interrogation, and when I told that name, rank and serial number was all I could give as he well knew, he then proceeded to tell me all about my outfit. My jeep had our Regiment number printed on it. He told me a bit of the history of the 101st Division, and who our CO was. (He was a couple months behind on that — didn't know that the CO he named had been killed in Holland.)

After he had interrogated the rest of the men, he called me back in, saying he couldn't sleep and would like to talk with me. He offered me coffee, but I said that I should like some very much if he were offering it to all the men with me, that I considered it very unfair treatment of Americans not to give them any food or water for nearly thirty-six hours. He regretted that no supplies or provisions had come through for them — we were too close to the front. He assured me that at our next stop we would be well fed — a German lie that was to get very monotonous during the next two weeks. At least, I insisted, he could get some bread and water for the men, which he finally and reluctantly did.

For three hours until dawn the interrogator amazed me with the strangest monologue I have ever listened to. He had been a merchant in Hamburg, had a family and delighted in showing me a hundred or more pictures of his wife and children, relatives, friends, etc. He spoke of the position of the Church in Germany — that it was the only stable and sensible organization in the world, and especially in the Fatherland. He himself had been surprised at the German break-through, but was convinced that it would peter out in a couple of weeks. He knew as all sensible Germans knew that Germany was beaten and had lost the war when she was driven out of Africa. America was more civilized than Germany, but Germany was more cultured than America. England was the real cause of the war, Russia the real menace to future civilization. Germans are home-loving, kindly, and unwarlike people, but the Nazi regime was ambitious — insanely so. Germany might have won the war, had its stupid leaders been content with Austria, Hungary, Slovakia, Poland, etc., and had they invaded England, which could have been done without great losses, and had Russia been left alone until England was defeated. Then a comparison of the various religions of the world, etc., etc. All this without asking me any questions or with any apparent effort to draw me out. I didn't get it. He finished by telling me that he was sick of war, and that he would be executed if the Gestapo knew what he had told me.

In the morning we started to march again… no breakfast. We stopped late that night at a rear area supply depot, and were given each a cold boiled potato and a little green apple. We slept in a tiny church, and were crowded enough to keep fairly warm. Again no breakfast the following morning, marched until dark — no dinner and no supper. We stayed in a barn where 400 other American prisoners were already cramped together trying to keep warm. That day American planes had come over in thousands — you can't imagine what a sight it was. We passed a German column moving up to the front, and as we did some P-47s began to strafe the column. Following our guards we dashed into the woods, and skirted the road for the next several miles. What a job those planes did — one after another vehicle would go up in flames and the German casualties were so great that we began to fear German reprisal action.

We had walked from Belgium, all the way across Luxembourg, and on the 24th of December we walked (without breakfast or dinner) to Prum in Germany. We were herded (800 of us by now) into the upstairs auditorium of a school where Hitler's and Goering's pictures covered the front wall. We were told that we were going to be fed — supper was being prepared now. We sort of expected that even the Germans would remember that this was Christmas eve. Our supper consisted of one half boiled turnip and a cup of warm water — nothing else. The men were in a mood to riot. I suggested to the colonel in charge (American colonel) that I hold service. It was a pitch-black night and the city was being bombed all night long (I hadn't known before that our fighter planes bombed at night). The Germans had placed us in the most dangerous place in the city — even a near-miss would collapse the building. We sang Silent Night with the roar of planes overhead and bombs dropping very close. I said a prayer, and then spoke for about a half hour on the idea that Christ is always where He is least expected to be — that He is just surely among us tonight as He was in the manger in Bethlehem nineteen hundred years ago. Though we may be thousands of miles from home, in enemy hands, cold and hungry — we have that which makes

Christmas Christmas, and He stretches forth His infant hand to each of us tonight as we kneel to adore Him.

Christmas Day we were given one slice of bread as we started on our way — no dinner and no supper. We marched about twenty miles to the town of Gerolstein. There was a group of 700 Americans about an hour ahead of us. All 1500 of us were pushed into a two-story building. But just before we went in American bombers came overhead. We prayed that they would keep on going and just as we thought they had passed us up without any unwelcome Christmas gift we heard the terrifying whistle of bombs falling. We hit the ground, just as the most terrific blasts you can imagine bounced us up in the air. They hit about 200 yards away but flying debris killed 8 and a direct hit on the group a couple hundred yards ahead of me killed, I believe, about 30 of our men and wounded others. Some of the bombs hit the local hospital in which we had several Americans. The Germans sent the wounded Americans down to our building, and although we were so packed in that we couldn't budge, let alone sit or lie down, we had to make room for a hundred wounded. I shall never forget it — the filth and misery of the place. A lieutenant with his leg blown off just below the hip told us to take care of the other men first. Our aid men had practically nothing left to care for the wounded, and the Germans laughed at requests. A number of men were sent out to clean up the bombed city, and they were abused unmercifully.

We were given nothing to eat that night, or the next morning, or the next afternoon. We were allowed out one at a time — 1500 of us. I was allowed out to bury the men in the local cemetery — the Germans were much more solicitous about the dead than they were about the living.

As I got back to the building I saw a German guard stop every American who came out. I watched for a bit before going back in. The guard offered a slice of bread for a wrist watch. I saw one American make the exchange and the German made the same offer to the next man. Finally an American came out who had a Parker pen but no watch. He offered that for the bread, and the German took the pen, tore the slice of bread in two and gave the American a half slice for it. That night the first group were sent down to the depot, which had been bombed that day, and were placed in boxcars and sealed in. It was still early evening, and a P-47 came over, strafed the railroad yards and killed eleven more men (Americans). Gerolstein will always remain in my mind as a city of misery. The next morning each man received a cup of soup, and a fifth of a loaf of bread and two inches of livenvurst. The Germans told us that this was to be our rations for two days, but every man was so starved that he bolted the whole ration almost at once.

We walked for the next two days from dawn till dark, and without food. American fighter planes would swoop down at us, but we stayed in formation and waved whatever we had. They would recognize us as Americans and tip their wings and wave and leave. Often as we approached a town it would be just getting a going-over by fighter planes and dive-bombers. We would have to wait at the edge of the town until it was over. You can be sure that we were not royally welcomed. I had an aircorps leather jacket on and a civilian seeing this ran up and cracked me with a shovel. It didn't hurt very much but I was careful to wear my trenchcoat over the leather jacket after that when we went through towns.

On our march through this part of Germany we saw dozens of buzz bombs take off from their camouflaged ramps on the other side of the hills that paralleled the road. They made a noise like a broken-down 1928 Dodge truck, and an orange flame poured out the rear end. They looked like giant birds with tails on fire. Not infrequently we could see ten or twelve in the air at the same time. I must say that they at least diverted our minds from our aching feet. The first time we saw a V-2 launched from a distance of several hundred yards it frightened all of us almost to death, including the guards. The buzz bomb (V-1) is to the V-2 as a 22 cal. shot is to a 155 mm. shell. These huge monsters of destruction took off with such a terrific roar that we thought at first that a giant plane was crashing at full speed right on top of us. Then followed a very loud swoosh — sh-shing sound, and we looked up to see a ten-thousand foot vapor serpent begin to dissolve slowly as the rocket, still visible many thousands of feet higher, gradually went out of sight. These rockets climbed more than sixty miles into the stratosphere before they began to descend with supersonic speed upon some unsuspecting section of England. Observation platforms, always crowded with civilians, were placed a few hundred yards from the launching sites. It must have been a tremendous boost to their wavering morale to know that they possessed such a mighty weapon of war.

On the second night out of Gerolstein we stopped at the little village of Bos. And here the townspeople went all out to feed us as best they could. Every housewife made soup and sandwiches and hot coffee (even ersatz coffee tasted good). These people were very kind, and when they found out that I was a priest they offered me anything they had. I couldn't quite understand why the people of that town were so different, until one of the women informed us that the town's Catholic pastor had told all his parishioners to do what they could for any prisoners who passed through.

Many of the men were getting footsore and had difficulty keeping up. We marched till dark, and were put in a warehouse, but it was so bitter cold that the guards decided to march us all night rather than try to sleep on the cement floor of that frame building. At three a. m. we arrived at Koblenz, and a more devastated city you cannot imagine. Another bomb dropped on it would simply have been wasted. This city of 400,000 was absolutely flat. We wandered around the streets for three hours trying to find a way out of town, but debris had blocked every street. Finally, holding each other's hands we had to walk carefully single file across the bombed and wrecked bridge on the Rhine. We had now walked twenty-four hours straight and we had had to drop many of the men at little village hospitals.

About ten kilometers beyond Koblenz we waited for three hours for our rations. Each man received a fifth of a loaf of bread, and then a large number of men shared a quart can of pressed meat. Then they pushed us on with no rest. It was sleeting and we were in wretched spirits and most of the men in very bad physical shape; every step from there on was in misery. At three in the afternoon we arrived absolutely exhausted at Bad Ems — well named, believe me. We felt that we could go no farther. But the townspeople would not have us; they refused to allow us to stay in the town stables, which had nothing in them but mighty inviting straw. They herded us in the park in the town square, and the people came in droves to ridicule us and laugh at us. The super-race really showed its true status then, and how contemptibly small it seemed to be.

How proud I was to be a member of that tired, worn-out group of Yanks. One of the men called for a prayer. Every man bowed his head as I led the prayer for strength and courage for all of us, and we finished with the Our Father. The hospital there was also the Corps Hdqs. (a violation of Geneva rules), and the German officers refused to speak or listen to our American colonel, and they sent a sergeant out to tell us to get moving. The colonel, one of the two doctors and a couple of majors were through — they had to be helped to the hospital. The rest, about 400 now, went on.

About twenty kilometers on to the next town, which turned out to be Limburg, and we were all finished; we could go no farther. They told us that there was a prison camp only three miles from town. This, we felt sure, must be our destination. Just then the air raid sirens sounded; it was the first warning. A few minutes later a different signal from the sirens indicated that the planes were definitely headed this way. Then came the signal to hit for the air raid shelters. The guards took all of us down one of these huge underground cement shelters. It had dozens of very large rooms deep and safe from anything but a block-buster. The Germans poured in by the hundreds: children and mothers with babes in arms, old folks and sick people, soldiers and ministers, police and prostitutes. There was no panic and everything was done with fine order, as though it had been a daily habit for years. But the look on these poor people's faces was enough to soften even our own bitterness into something like sympathy and compassion. They regarded us with neither fear nor hatred; nor did it seem to occur to them to enjoy seeing us subject to a bombing from our own planes. One of the pilots in our group told me that had he been able really to envision the misery suffered by the poor people of the town he bombed, he would never have been able to do it. Then the planes came over. Limburg was apparently not their target for that night. They passed over the city dropping only five bombs as a token that the city was not forgotten and would be taken care of later.

When we came out of the shelter we were told that Limburg was absolutely filled up with prisoners. Major Saunders, the ranking prisoner, told the chief guard that we were incapable of walking further; we must stop here, and would be glad to sleep in the air raid shelters. The chief guard went to get instructions; it was three hours before he returned. We were desolate because we were not taken to the Limburg Stalag, but we little realized then how fortunate it was for us that they had no more room. Two days after this, New Year's Day, 1945, the German newspapers and radio carried the story of the bombing of Limburg, and took great delight in describing how one American plane flying above the low fog that covered the town and the nearby Stalag dropped five bombs on the prison camp, killing more than sixty American officers. Nor was this just propaganda. It was verified by men transferred from Limburg to Neu-brandenburg, our prison home. The American press and radio likewise verified the story months later.

At last, after walking over 185 miles in the last ten days, they put us in boxcars — sixty men to a French 40 and 8 car (40 and 8 means that it can hold 40 men or 8 horses.) And now (I know that you will find it difficult to believe) we were sealed in these cars for six days and six nights, without a single bite to eat or a drop of water to drink! That seems incredible, but I have 400 witnesses to the fact. There were two little openings at each end of the car. We took turns sitting in each other's laps, for there was no room to sit down. Our hunger during those first three days seemed more than we could stand. All I could think of was Aunt Millie's rolls and homemade bread and bacon and eggs at 821 West 6th St. The men couldn't seem to stop talking about food. Everyone became very irritable at times, but generally speaking the men took this hunger trial in stride. We would take turns reaching to scrape the snow off the top of the boxcar. Once, while stopping in a town, we called to a woman to bring us some water. We threw four helmets out to her to bring it in. She came back carrying the water and a fourteen or fifteen-year-old boy helping her. She had just reached us when a guard saw her. He ran up, dumped our water on the ground, and gave the woman a push. The boy went down to the other end of the car to hoist up the water quickly, but he was not quick enough. By this time the chief guard came up, and the two of them pushed the boy against a brick retaining wall and gave him a beating. This stuff sounds hackneyed and like a second-rate Hollywood version of Germany, and had someone told this to me a year ago I would have laughed at such "propaganda."

New Years Day I held what passed for a service in our crowded car, and every man present made resolutions, which I am sure, will be more lasting and carry more weight than the usual New Years resolutions. As for myself, every Christmas and New Years from now on will mean so much more to me than it ever did before. After the third day I didn't seem to be quite so hungry, and the last couple of days it didn't bother me at all. This was the case with the rest of the men too. You can actually get used to going without food.

We didn't know where we were going. We had passed through Berlin, and were heading north. I discovered later that many of us had the same thoughts, but didn't dare to mention it. We had begun to suspect that the Germans were intentionally starving us to death, and that we would not be brought out of the boxcars alive. But on the sixth day, during a driving blizzard, we were let out of the cars, and told that we had arrived at our destination, Neubrandenburg, Mecklenburg. We were terribly weak, of course, and it was all we could do to walk the four miles to Stalag II-A — our home for the duration. On the way we ate fistfuls of snow, and ice cream never tasted half so good.

Immediately upon arriving at the Stalag we were sent to the showers and delousing building. The shower brought our spirits up immediately. Looking at my own body I could scarcely believe that it was mine. Normally heavy men looked skinny and thin men looked like skeletons. We had to laugh at each other, for we certainly were a sorry-looking lot. All the officers' heads were shaved — to humiliate us I assume, or to make us more conspicuous if we escaped. The enlisted men did not have their heads shaved. The men began to perk up quickly. That is something that will always remain a mystery to the Germans — the American sense of humor. American soldiers are a great lot — they gripe and complain about every little thing in garrison life, where things are quite comfortable. But when the going gets rough, and they really suffer, then they take it without a moan. It seems like a strange thing, but it is a fact that the more difficult and trying the circumstances are the higher the morale is.

Eating, that almost forgotten experience, was next. They brought in buckets of soup — grass soup with a few turnips in it and lots and lots of little worms. But the only complaint we had, as one GI remarked, was that the worms weren't fat enough. We guzzled it — and them — greedily.

CHAPTER VIII: LIFE IN PRISON CAMP

Stalag II-A, we soon discovered, was a camp for enlisted men only, and we officers had been sent there by mistake. The German Commandant of the camp told us that we would remain for a couple of days and then would be marched to the officers camp about two hundred kilometers away. The American "Man of Confidence" (the title given to the soldier that the Americans selected to represent them to the German authorities) came to me and asked whether I would be willing to stay at this Stalag since there were between five and six thousand Americans there without any officer or chaplain. I was glad to accept, but the Germans were unwilling that any officer remain in an enlisted men's camp, although the Geneva Convention Articles clearly prescribe that prisoners of war shall have the services of their own chaplains if such are available. The Germans couldn't see it that way however, so the resourceful "Man of Confidence" had recourse to other means to bring about the desired end. He contacted the Serbian doctor who had been of tremendous help to the American sick and wounded. The Serb doctor examined me, and diagnosed a case of double pneumonia. Tired and weak as I was I found it quite easy to act the part of the patient. After the rest of the officers were marched out of the camp a couple of days later I made a quick recovery, and, despite certain misgivings of the German Commandant, was permitted to remain at the camp until the end of the war. The Commandant even obliged me by granting an Ausweis (pass) and freedom of all the various compounds within the camp.

"Man of Confidence" not only represents the prisoners' complaints to the German authorities, but likewise acts as the commander of the prisoners, and provides for good order within the compound. Sergeant Hilary Lucas handled this difficult job with as much tact and efficiency, I believe, as any officer could have done. He was extremely fortunate in his selection of men to help him in the command of the three thousand Americans; his "barracks chiefs" and other men given authority by him had a way of getting things done without seeming to throw their weight around by ordering other enlisted men to do this or do that. They obtained maximum co-operation with a minimum of friction. I have seen many officers in the army do far worse.

Two American doctors were left at the camp at different times, but were denied the permission to visit the Lazaret (hospital) where the prison's seriously ill were kept. Not until just before our liberation was Dr. Cecil B. Hawes, Captain, allowed to treat Americans and British in the Lazaret.

If you have ever seen one of our prison camps for German PW's in the United States don't get the idea that you know what a camp for American PW's in Germany is like. The only similarity is the high fence, the coils of barbed wire and the guard towers. Aside from these essentials of any PW camp, the difference is greater than between Park Avenue and Mott Street. The filth of the camp strikes one at first as appalling, but one seems to get more or less numb to it as time goes in, and it still remains a mystery to me why typhus and typhoid epidemics did not occur. The camp had separate compounds for the Serbs,

Dutch, Poles, French, Italians, Belgians, Russians, Americans, and British. In all there were about eighty thousand prisoners registered in the camp, but about half of these were out in working groups and never returned to the camp except to bring in the sick.

The first week or so of prison life still seems more like a dream to me than reality. I had seen the German PW camp at Camp Forest, and had expected about the same thing in Germany, without the same quality or quantity of food, of course. What I found is common knowledge now, for newspapers and newsreels have not spared the American public's sensibilities regarding this necessary bit of education. The weather was bitter cold and the suffering intense. The Americans had been in the camp only about five months and consequently were in far better shape than the other prisoners, some of whom had been there for over five years. The daily food ration per man consisted of a bowl of soup (so-called), a tenth of a loaf of bread, and a cup of tea which the men used for shaving water, for they couldn't drink it. Four days a week each man received a couple of potatoes. The soup was invariably either cabbage (with worms) or rotten turnips (with worms). The men of course were very thin, and many of them became sick and died. Fortunately for all of us, Red Cross parcels came through after I was there a short time.

One of the first things I wanted to do was contact the priests in the camp. There were six priests in the French compound, two Dutch priests, and an Italian and a Polish priest. Each of them greeted me with sincere warmth, and together they rounded up Mass equipment for me. Many of the French or Poles worked downtown (Neu-brandenburg) for which they were compensated, and they were able to bribe the guards to get wine and hosts from the local

German priest. The French had also made a very devotional and artistic chapel out of one of their barracks. All the French priests had been enlisted men in the French army and consequently had to work for the Germans. The oldest among them, however, was a very wonderful man with the charm and kindliness of a St. Francis de Sales. His thick hair was long and white, as was his neatly trimmed beard. The Germans seemed to respect him, and he was given freedom of the camp. The rest of us priests considered ourselves his curates, and I received tremendous help from his kindly advice and priestly example. We spent may enjoyable evenings together. Though no one was permitted to go out of the barracks after eight p. m., I would frequently sneak out to visit M. l'Abbe in his barracks, and we would talk most of the night, using a goulash of his bad English, my worse French, our questionable Latin, and pidgin German. Our desperate efforts to express ourselves so delighted the old priest one night that he let out a loud laugh, and a guard passing by came to the window and turned his flashlight on us. The old priest reassured him.

A shipment of boxes labeled "Red Cross" and addressed to American Prisoners of War arrived at the camp one day. The men grouped about those huge cartons thinking that at last food had arrived. Weak and emaciated as they were, they anticipated a real treat of good American food. You can imagine their pathetic feelings when the cartons were opened only to reveal their useless contents… football shoulder-pads, tennis racquets, and other items for which we had neither the space nor the energy to waste in their use.

This disappointing shipment, however, was followed a week later by the arrival of Red Cross food parcels, and other shipments kept us pretty well stocked for the duration of the war. You might be interested in what a food parcel contains: three small cans of pressed meat, a can of salmon or tuna fish, a can of cheese, a can of powdered milk, two bars of real chocolate, a box of sugar squares, a can of soluble coffee, a box of raisins, vitamin tablets, a box of crackers, a can of oleo or butter, and, most precious of all (especially for their bartering value), five packages of cigarettes. Each man was issued a parcel per week, and we shared our parcels with the British in the camp, alloting them one parcel per man each week.

Through our food parcels we became the aristocracy of the camp. Even the Germans were not eating as well as we were in some respects. Our coffee, chocolate, and cigarettes were especially desired by the Germans, and bartering and trading became the most intriguing and profitable occupation in the American compound. German guards could scarcely restrain their enthusiasm for American cigarettes, and since the demand was so great on their part for our luxuries, which we had in some abundance, it became expedient that we set up our own OPA price scale to prevent an inflation and a cheapening of our own goods.

To maintain our cigarettes and coffee at the highest possible worth we computed and posted our trade value in this manner:

Kriegies: Observe this price scale, and keep the value of cigarettes up!

For 1 two-lb. loaf of bread — give no more than 10 cigarettes or ½ chocolate bar.

For a 2 lb. sack of flour — give no more than 15 cigarettes.

For 1 doz. eggs — give no more than 25 cigarettes or 1 chocolate bar.

For 1 good chicken — give no more than 1 small can of soluble coffee.

For 12 large onions — give no more than 12 cigarettes or ½ chocolate bar.

For 1 good pair of gloves — give no more than 15 cigarettes.

For 1 lb. beefsteak — give no more than 25 cigarettes or 1 chocolate bar.

By and large the Americans stuck pretty close to the price scale, except when they could strike an even better bargain, which of course was not contrary to our OPA intentions. Despite the manner in which American GIs squander their money when they have plenty, they are still the world's best traders and keenest bargain-makers when they have little to give in exchange. All this probably strikes you as very amusing, and, as I reflect upon it, it tickles me to think of the German guards smuggling various food items past their own guards to get in exchange the coveted American cigarettes, chocolate or coffee. But believe me, the actual bartering was a serious matter between the Germans and the Americans. And I doubt whether the Wall Street wizards have juggled millions of bushels of wheat with greater self-interested cunning than a Kriegie wielded his mighty cigarette to his own advantage.

Since there were no Pure Food Laws within the camp the GI never scrupled to mislabel or misrepresent his article. One night I recall that a German guard came into the barracks and produced a fine hen from under his "great coat" (the "great coat" worn by guards is a huge garment that hangs all the way to the ground and is large enough for two men). He wanted one of our tiny cans of soluble coffee and fifteen cigarettes for his hen. The GIs felt they could do better. (Usually three or four Americans would buy something like this together and would pick the sharpest fellow to do the trading.) This particular American haggled and argued with the guard for well over an hour until the exasperated German finally agreed to trade his hen for the coffee and to forget the cigarettes. The matter having been settled, the articles were exchanged. The American felt the chicken critically and the German sniffed the coffee suspiciously. They parted, each quite satisfied that he had made a good bargain. About twenty minutes later the German came back... angry, fuming, and spouting German faster than my untrained ear could follow. I asked him what the matter was. It seemed that the can of coffee he had received for his hen turned out to be in reality just a can of sand with a sprinkling of coffee on top. Realizing the impossibility of locating the swindler, the German had to content himself with a few anti-Semitic invectives against all Americans.

I was very anxious to organize a good religious program for the American and British compounds. We set aside one corner of a barracks for a chapel sanctuary, and we employed the very considerable artistic talent in the camp to make this corner as beautiful and as devotional as our limited tools and materials permitted. We were able to bribe the guards for the lumber necessary to build an altar. Several scarlet blankets were obtained by the same means. The altar was built on a platform with three steps leading to it. The blankets were cut to make an antependium and a backdrop for the crucifix which was carved out of a block of wood by an Italian prisoner. By our usual means of a bribe we obtained from a German guard paper and a complete set of pastel crayons. With these the Serbian artist did a magnificent job on the Stations of the Cross. By means of a couple more chocolate bars we got two more scarlet blankets with which we covered the crude Communion rail. With the material left over we made a canopy for the altar. An American Jewish boy painted a lovely Madonna and a picture of St. Joseph for the sides of the altar. A German guard became interested in the project and obtained wiring material and a socket was placed behind the canopy. When the light was turned on the effect was so satisfying that I question whether any priest ever gazed upon his church with greater satisfaction and joy than did I upon our humble prison sanctuary. It became very truly a spiritual oasis for our homesick boys. Many a lad during our long days, weeks, and months of imprisonment found relief there in a quiet prayer. Many found there the fulfillment of our Lord's promise, "Come unto me… and I will refresh you."

A couple of men also built a small room for me adjoining our little chapel, and I was there able to have the privacy necessary for confessions and consultations. Each day most of the Catholics attended Mass, although I was forced to limit Communions to Sunday only, because of the difficulty of obtaining hosts. We had no large hosts at all and used the small ones for Mass and quartered these on Sunday for communicants. Twice a week I held a non-denominational service for the Protestant men. Religion was a constant subject of conversation and the entire credit for the large number of converts belongs to several Catholic men who knew their religion, knew how to present it properly, and knew how to live it well. One young fellow in a nearby working camp instructed and baptized nine men, although he had never been beyond the first year of high school himself. A check proved that his instructions had been thorough and his converts solid Catholics.

So strong was the German feeling towards Jews that they even separated the Jewish American prisoners from the rest of us despite the vigorous protest by our "Man of Confidence" and myself. These men were sent out as working crew, and were treated no worse than the other crews, but we feared possible reprisals against them as the war drew to a close. Even when the Red Cross officials protested to the German authorities nothing was done about this segregation. The Germans carried their Jew-hatred to such a ridiculous extreme that no Red Cross articles with Jewish names on them were allowed to get into the camp. We had a beat-up old phonograph, but all the records sent to us had a Jewish name on them, either as composer, orchestra, producer, or manufacturer. Even Irving Berlin's "White Christmas" was smashed in the censor's office. The only record to come through was "Into Each Life Some Rain Must Fall..."1 often prayed that someone would drop that record and break it, but nobody ever did. It was a pity the Germans hadn't smashed that one too.

The entertainment in the camp was homespun, but really quite good on the whole and varied enough to interest everyone. For violations of discipline, lack of cleanliness, etc., the Man of Confidence imposed fines... forfeiture of some parcel item from a cigarette to a can of coffee, depending upon the gravity of the offense. With these fines musical instruments and other entertainment materials were bought from the Germans. (Incidentally, the Chaplain's fund... to pay for hosts and wine... was constantly augmented by the contribution of one cigarette exacted from any man I caught using bad language.) A hill-billy quartet was only too willing to entertain at any time of the day or night. They were indefatigable and their repertoire inexhaustible. Another man, "Chick" by name, had had considerable experience in vaudeville, and the shows he organized and put on were very clever and great morale builders. The shows became a bit ribald at times and I had to needle "Chick" occasionally, but he took it well and tried to co-operate, although he couldn't control the asides and the adlibs.

One night "Chick" staged a minstrel in the barracks. The makeups and costumes were masterpieces of Yank ingenuity. Most of the jokes and songs were racy and crudely insulting digs at the Germans. It so happened that a couple dozen guards got wind of the show and came to see it. They sat there and laughed and laughed at every joke and song. The colored costumes with bright ties tickled them to death. The Americans were pretty apprehensive until they saw that the Germans didn't understand a word or catch any of the insinuations. Then the GIs got a big wallop out of that... the Germans laughing at the show, and the Americans laughing at the Germans who didn't know that they were being ribbed. I was more than a little relieved when the show was over, and the Germans slapped the members of the cast on the back and muttered something about Americans being "good comrades."

The best of the entertainers, however, was a string quartet. The violinist had played for years in the Boston Symphony — with a name like Elephtherios Elephtherokos what else could he be but a musician... or possibly a wrestler? The bass viol player and the guitar player had studied their instruments for years and were excellent. The vocalist, a cadaverous Sinatra-appearing lad, had a soft dreamy voice, and had sung for several name bands in the States. The total effect was quite professional.

One of the most interesting characters in the camp was Zaza. Zaza was a little Italian boy who was brought to the camp when he was only two and a half years old. His parents had been killed in a bombing early in the war. An Italian soldier had picked him up and taken him to the camp. So Zaza had been reared in this abnormal environment. He never had known or played with other children, and his manners were very grown-up. The stocky little fellow looked like a midget Mussolini, although he couldn't tolerate being called "Mussolini." Zaza in this strange environment had matured way beyond his years; he fixed his own bunk, went to bed and got up when he chose, washed his own clothes, and prepared his own food. He was given freedom of the entire camp, and he could speak fluent Italian, Polish, German, and French, and could get along fairly well in English. I once asked him if he would like to come to the United States with me. He rubbed his chin for a minute and then said in English, "I think America be vera vera nice, but Italy want us there, many things to build in Italy when war is over." I never ceased to be astounded by his mature outlook, but I fear his abnormal childhood will result in later emotional crises.

One day I went to the bathhouse to take a shower (a unique privilege the German Commandant had granted me). The German in charge, however, said that there was no water. On my way back to the American compound I met Zaza, who had the same bathhouse privilege. "Whasa mat?" he asked. "The Heinie says 'no water.'" I replied.

Zaza laughed, "He is liar," and he went into the bath house. I waited to have a laugh at Zaza's disappointment. Pretty soon Zaza stuck his head out the window and called, "Come, didn't I say he is liar?" We both had a good shower.

The saddest part of prison life was the lack of the bare essentials for medical care. Quite a number of Americans and British had arrived at the camp with frozen feet. The Serbian and the Polish doctor did everything they could and worked with heroic patience and skill, but they were hopelessly handicapped by lack of supplies. Five men had to have both their legs amputated and eighteen had one leg amputated. Many wounded men were serious gangrene cases, and the Lazaret was filled with pneumonia and dysentery patients. Some of these poor boys died. The Polish doctor would sometimes actually cry when he was forced to use toilet paper as compresses and newspaper for bandages. The wounded and the sick were cared for by our medical aid men with the greatest solicitude and, I might add, with unashamed love. Nothing, I believe, refines men's characters so much, or makes men so Christ-like, patient, and self-sacrificing, as caring for the sick and the helpless. The Polish and the Serbian doctors will always remain in my mind as the finest Christian examples of a profession second only to the priesthood in the dignity and greatness of its mission.

We buried an average of two Americans and two British a week. All of the Catholics were anointed and received Viaticum (a French priest had provided me with an oil-stock). The Protestant men readily said the Acts of Faith, Hope, Charity, and Contrition after me, and, I have no doubt, were very well received by Him who also died a prisoner. The Germans as usual were more solicitous toward the dead than they were toward the living. We were allowed to take eight pallbearers and an honorary group of twelve men to escort each body from the hospital (about a half mile from the camp) to the cemetery. The pallbearers carried the body in its wooden coffin on their shoulders. As the procession passed the camp on its way to the cemetery on the hill everyone in the camp turned toward the procession, paused and saluted the deceased, a small act that never failed to impress me deeply. After the burial ritual I always felt obliged to say a few words to those in attendance… usually something like this: "Though we bury our comrade-in-arms here in six feet of foreign soil; though thousands of miles from his home and unattended by his family and friends; though he be buried naked in this crude coffin; and though his Prisoner of War tag remain with him still, nailed to a crude marker; these are superficial and relatively unimportant things. The important thing is that in the supreme moment of his life he was given the grace of a holy and Christian death; the important thing is that he has been liberated by his Saviour's love from the prison of this life. Today we represent his family, his country and his Church. As his family would wish we offer up our prayers for his soul. His country, we remind ourselves, must ever be grateful for the price he paid for our freedom. His Church recognizes here a sacrifice closely linked to the sacrifice of the Crucified." Taps were blown and we returned to the camp.

Out of the twenty-one thousand Russians that had been registered in the camp eighteen thousand died, most of them of starvation. Everyday the pitiful sight of a wagonload of naked corpses on its way to cemetery hill made us Americans mighty grateful for citizenship in a "grasping Capitalistic country that has no regard for the masses." Believe me, the Russians that survived needed no argument other than the sight of our Red Cross parcels to convince them that there was something mighty phony about Uncle Joe and the government of the proletariat.

The hatred of the Germans for the Russians was incredible. The Russian dead were buried in pits, five hundred to a pit. On one occasion when I was burying an American and a couple of British men a Russian corpse had mistakenly been placed along side of the other three, and all four bodies were buried in coffins. When the Germans discovered the mistake the next day they dug up the Russian and dumped his body into the pit for the Russian dead. Many Russians were buried while still breathing. It was also a common thing for the Russians to keep their dead with them for days so that the dead man's rations could be drawn from the kitchen, and at roll call the dead would be held upright by the men on each side in the close, tight formation. Authentic cases of cannibalism occurred among the Russians. Horrible as this sounds I have come to believe that there is nothing that a starving man will not do, and who can say that these poor creatures were responsible for their actions? I know that this sounds like Hollywood wartime propaganda at its worst, but there are hundreds of American soldiers who can substantiate every word.

A little Russian boy fourteen years old was caught stealing potatoes from the kitchen. The German guard made the lad lie flat on the ground and stretch out his arms, and the guard shot him through each hand. One of the American aid men cared for the boy's wounds and we collected some food for him. A couple of weeks later our "Man of Confidence" managed to get the boy into our infirmary (so-called) and when his wounds healed somewhat he remained to help our own aid men. He carried bed pans, washed and shaved the sick, scrubbed the place regularly, and became devoted to the Americans. I have never seen a happier boy in my life than when some Red Cross clothing came in, and we fitted the lad in an American uniform.

Not many Americans attempted escape, and those who did attempt it were unsuccessful. We were guarded closely (except toward the very end of the war), and no one was allowed out of the barracks at night. We had also seen the German police clogs go after a crazed Russian who had desperately tried to squirm and dig under the fence. Of the twenty or so Americans who tried to escape none was successful, and three were killed by the Gestapo. We were several hundred miles in the interior of Germany, and the people were jittery and armed to fight the expected American and Russian airborne landings in the interior of Germany.

About the first of March the Swiss Red Cross representatives arrived at the Camp to hear our complaints against the German treatment and to make the proper adjustments. Incidentally, the Germans, upon the arrival of the Red Cross men, served the camp prisoners the first palatable soup we had seen, and even gave every man a double ration of bread, a ration of sugar, jam, potatoes, and two inches of bologna. The Swiss failed to help the prisoners very much, but one thing they did do that I appreciated was to get a pass for me to leave the camp to visit American working groups within a radius of a hundred miles. I availed myself of this privilege to the utmost, and I kept a guard busy constantly escorting me on a bicycle about the country. The guard would invariably want to visit friends or relatives on these trips, and in this way I became quite well acquainted with many German families. The German families seemed to me to be very closely knit units with most if not all the virtues of hard-working Christian people. I am quite convinced that they were in great part ignorant of the atrocities perpetrated upon the conquered peoples. They did not condone the evils they saw in their government, but by nature the German people seem to have an exaggerated respect for authority, no matter how unworthy that authority might be. Fear, too, was obviously a deterrent from any expressions of dissatisfaction with those in power. The people treated me kindly and with respect and reverence, and everyone of them seemed to think that I ought to know this or that relative in America, for the relative had prospered greatly. The American working groups that I visited on these trips were making out much better than the boys in the camp, for rations were far better. They too had received Red Cross parcels and were able to barter not only with the guards, but with civilians as well.

An American Colonel who had become sick on a prisoner march from Poland was left at Stalag II-A about the middle of March and remained for two weeks. He was a very clever man, and during the first few days in the camp he was able to have a radio smuggled in piece by piece. We had tried this before but had never been able to assemble a complete radio. He told us that the BBC was broadcasting instructions every week to prisoners of war, and as the war drew to a close it was essential that we comply with these orders.

The great problem was to find a suitable place to hide the radio, for the Gestapo each month made a thorough inspection of every barracks. They would pull up the floor boards, take the bunks apart, and probe the ground around and under the barracks — in short they did their job thoroughly and well. Finally an idea dawned upon me that might offer security for our radio. I had a boy build a little pulpit for my chapel, and he did a masterful job in fixing a little trap door on the top. He then covered the whole thing with a piece of the scarlet blanket material, and inserted a long spike into a hole that kept the trap door tight. By pulling out the nail the door would fly open and the radio could be used. The first time we tuned in on the BBC, a chill ran up and down my spine. It almost seemed like our liberation.

Of course we had to use the radio with the utmost caution, and could not even let our own Americans know that we had it. The reason for the secrecy with our own men was that the Germans had a "plant" among us, that is, a German who had been in America, who spoke perfect English, and about whom we would have no suspicion. A "plant" is a common means for the detaining government to pick up valuable information dropped by prisoners of war, and also a very effective means of preventing escapes. We had our suspicions as to who the "plant" was, but we were never sure until the last couple weeks of the war when he was so careless one night as to talk in his sleep. The information came through perfectly as to what we were to do during the last few weeks of the war, and this knowledge proved of tremendous value.

One Sunday morning shortly before our liberation a very embarrassing thing happened. It was during Mass and I was just about to begin the sermon. I had forgotten to put the spike back securely in the trap door, and as I rested my arm on the pulpit and quoted my sermon text: "Seek ye first the kingdom of God, and all these things shall be added unto you," the trap door flew open and the radio dropped out in front of all the men. There was a long three seconds of silence and then the place broke into a roar. It was with considerable embarrassment that I recovered the radio and stuffed it back into the pulpit, and tried to compose myself and restore order. The constant snickering made it very difficult to concentrate on the sermon, and after about five painful minutes I gave it up as a bad job, and went on with the Mass. The worst part of the accident was the presence in the congregation of two German guards, but when both of them went to Communion I felt pretty sure that they would say nothing. These two guards had been very decent and quite helpful on many occasions. Just before our liberation when all the German soldiers were taking off towards the west to escape the Russians and to surrender to the Americans I gave each of these two guards a note to the Americans who picked them up that they had been friendly and helpful to American prisoners of war. Whether it helped them or not I haven't any idea.

I think that I shall always remember vividly and joyfully Easter in Stalag 11-A, and I believe everyone who was there will remember it as long as he lives. Good Friday had been observed by Catholics and Protestants alike in the American compound with the Stations of the Cross and an hour's meditation taken from the Imitation of Christ... the Chapter on the Royal Road of the Holy Cross. The French priest had managed to have a set of dalmatics smuggled in, and we prepared, without the Germans' knowledge, to hold an outdoor Solemn High Mass. The guard crew had been reduced to a skeleton force by this time, for every German under sixty had been sent to the front. Each nation was to be represented on the altar, and each nation had a little choir to sing part of the Mass, with the principal parts to be sung by all the choirs together. We hoped and prayed for a good day and it turned out perfect.

The wonderful saintly old French priest was the celebrant of the Mass. I was the deacon, the Dutch priest was subdeacon, an Italian priest was master of ceremonies, the Polish priest was assistant master of ceremonies, the Belgian "Man of Confidence" was thurifer, and for acolytes we had a Serb, a Scotsman, an American, and a Russian (the old French priest told me that this Russian was a saint). Two French priests directed and coordinated the choirs. About half an hour before the Mass, word was sent to the various compounds to assemble in the big field beside the kitchen. The Germans were too bewildered to make much of a protest, and besides war was so close to being over that they were very anxious to be friendly. All of the Catholics in the camp and many of the non-Catholics attended, and the number was well up in the thousands, the largest congregation I have ever seen apart from a national Eucharistic Congress. The crowd entirely surrounded the altar and what a sight it was. Many of the Germans were there, not as guards but as worshipers. This was the Catholic Church; here were Frenchmen kneeling next to Serbs, next to Poles, Americans worshiping beside Belgians, beside Italians, Scotsmen finding the bond of brotherhood in the Mass with the Dutch, with Germans and with Russians. There was no argument here, no friction, no hatred, no intrigue or struggle for balance of power. Here was the Christ being elevated again, and drawing all things to Himself. Here was a King whom all could love and obey, and in that love and obedience find the happiness and freedom every man longs for. These were the thoughts of the brief sermon which was preached in four languages by four ministers of the Mass, in French, in English, in Italian, and in Polish. Do you wonder that I shall never forget that Easter? Hundreds of men went to Communion at that Mass, and I believe every American Catholic received. After the Mass the French priest had a little party for the priests and the servers, and it was then that he paid the finest compliment to American Catholics that I have ever heard. "You Americans," he said, "are the world's greatest lovers of the Eucharist."

Shortly after this we heard the tragic news of President Roosevelt's death. I held a solemn memorial service, and every nationality in the camp sent its highest ranking representative to attend. Later in the day a formation of all American and British in the camp was held, at which the representatives of the various nationalities extended their sympathies to the Americans and extolled the virtues of our past great leader. I said a prayer for the divine help and guidance of his successor. Taps were blown and the formation was dismissed. It was amazing to see the profound effect President Roosevelt's passing had upon the men.

We knew the day of liberation could not be far away. Russian artillery could be heard in the distance, and German civilians were evacuating Neu-brandenburg, traveling on anything that had wheels. Confusion and terror among the civilians and the retreating German wounded was the order of the day. I thought I had almost become emotionally numb to the sight of suffering and death, but the events of the next several days were to instill in me an even greater disgust and abhorrence for war than I had before.

CHAPTER IX: LIBERATION BY THE RUSSIANS

Each night during the month of April I would slip out of my room after the men had gone to sleep, and would take the radio out of its hiding place in the pulpit. While a couple of boys kept watch at the door of the barracks, the American "Man of Confidence" and I listened to the BBC for Allied instructions to prisoners of war. Our instructions were few but specific, and were broadcast in code. An Englishman, a sergeant from the G2 section of the British Airborne, listened with us. He knew the code, and deciphered it almost as fast as it was given. We were not to make any premature attempt at mass break or escape, for it would be foolish to lose lives now with assured freedom so close at hand. If the German guards fled, the ranking officer or non-commissioned officer was to take charge of the discipline and order of the group. "P.W." was to be painted in large block letters on top of each barracks, as were the Russian symbols for prisoner of war. A large "P.W." was to be marked out with stones or anything recognizable from the air in the largest open space in the prison camp. Any prisoner violence against German civilians was strictly forbidden, and German soldiers turning themselves over to Allied prisoners were to be held and given over to the force that liberated the camp. Every precaution was to be taken to avoid prisoner casualties of battles that might take place near and about the camp. Allied flags were to be flown above the camp as soon as the Germans were helpless to prevent it. Each night that we listened to the radio, the Russian artillery's muffled "woompf woompf" in the distance became more and more distinct, coming closer and closer.

Russian planes flew over the city of Neu-brandenburg and over the camp and dropped thousands of leaflets designed to terrify the German civilians; which they did very effectively. One of the pamphlets simply stated in German, "Rokosovski is at your gates." The reputation of Rokosovski's army was enough to panic the Germans, and the roads were soon jammed with German wagons loaded with the most cherished of family possessions, with children and old people, heading west hoping to escape the Russians, and preferring anything to falling into their hands.

Many of the guards in the camp deserted, and fled in the direction of the American lines. Some of these asked me for letters to their future captors, stating how kind they had been to the Americans. A few of these had been decent, and a couple of them actually ran great risks to help us. To these I gave notes telling how they had aided us, and I sincerely hope that this benefitted them. About a dozen guards, including the camp Commandant, turned themselves over to the prisoners and were locked up in the stone "block-house." The small garrison of the town dug in and prepared to defend it. We were busy digging trenches to take cover in as soon as the Russians began to shell the town. The events of the next few days were as terrible as I have ever seen or hope to see.

About midnight of April 28, the Russian tanks started coming in; the roar of the tanks coming from all sides was terrific. The opposition that the Germans were able to put up was almost totally ineffectual; as a matter of fact, the Russian infantry riding on the tanks (about fifteen or twenty to a tank) killed almost as many of their own men as they did the Germans. A couple of tanks, as they rolled into town, pushed down barbed wire fences and the guard towers of the prison camp. The Russian soldiers seemed to be wild men; with "squeeze-boxes" and banjos strapped to their backs, and firing their rifles and tommy-guns in every direction, they looked more like the old Mexico revolutionaries out on a spree than the army of one of the great powers of the world. Most of these soldiers were oriental or Mongolian in appearance.

Within an hour after their arrival, Neu-brandenburg was a sea of flames, which rose higher and higher as the night passed. It burned all the next day and there was scarcely a building that was not razed to the ground; the Catholic Church, strangely enough, was almost the only large building preserved. The Germans had a large army hospital about a quarter of a mile from the prison camp and it was packed with wounded; it was the first building set afire, although I was unable to find out for sure whether the wounded had been removed or not. The heat from the burning city became intense and lighted the camp as brightly as daylight. The Americans kept calm and in perfect order during this time — something that could not be said for the French, Italians, and Serbs, who bolted the camp in mobs and went to loot the city. The Russian prisoners of war, of whom there were only 3,000 remaining alive out of 21,000 that had been registered in the camp, were quite oddly the only prisoners not particularly happy to be liberated. Each of them was tossed a rifle and told to get up to the front quickly. The Russian army doesn't believe that those who surrender to the enemy should be treated humanely. The Russian doctor and several others who were accused by their fellow prisoners as collaborators with the Germans were immediately shot. The German Commandant of the camp was taken up the hill to the cemetery, forced to dig a hole and was shot and his body dumped into it.

The next day a Russian General came to the camp. He asked for the American in charge, and the boys brought him to my room. I offered the General a cigar, a couple of boxes of which had recently come through under the Red Cross label. The General thoroughly enjoyed the cigar and the coffee I served him. I sent for an American soldier who spoke Russian, and the conversation with the General became very interesting and enlightening. He said that the cigar was the best he had ever smoked and the coffee by far the best he ever drank. After trying one of his own cigarettes I had no cause to distrust the compliment. He said that he would send "something good" up to me. A Russian soldier brought that "something" up the next day. It turned out to be a big crockery jug of vodka, one whiff of which was more than enough for me. The General told me how sorrowful all Russians were that President Roosevelt had died, that they considered him a great friend of Russia. He praised American equipment very highly, and said that in his opinion the Russians could not have held out had it not been for American help in equipping the Russian Army. This was obviously true, for almost every piece of equipment that we saw the Russians use was American; they used Sherman tanks for the most part, and our two-and-a-half ton trucks, our jeeps, and our armored cars were all employed almost exclusively. The Russian fighter planes were all Bell Airacobras, a plane that American pilots considered obsolete and refused to fly. During the course of our conversation the General drank at least ten cups of coffee, and showed no signs of quitting until I had emptied the second pot in his cup.

A political commissar was brought into the camp, and he immediately called a meeting of the ranking officers of all the nationalities in the camp. He was a fine looking man, well mannered, and extremely intelligent — one of the best linguists that I have ever heard. He told us that we would remain in the camp until contact was made with the American lines. He gave us our instructions in French, Italian, Polish, Dutch, and in flawless English. He likewise said that our countries would be notified immediately that we had been liberated; the Americans (and only the Americans) might write one letter apiece to their families and these would be flown to American lines; food would be provided in abundance; transportation would be provided as soon as contact was made with American lines in this sector of Germany. He said that he was leaving a Russian Colonel in charge of the camp, and that all our needs would be satisfied, but that no one was to leave the camp without a pass. I asked him for a pass in order to round up any Americans who were in working groups in or near Neu-brandenburg. This he readily granted.

The old French priest came over and asked me to go downtown with him, for he wanted to see how the German priest and the German people who had not fled were making out. I certainly admired the old man's courage; he apparently feared no one. Expecting the worst, we were still shocked beyond words by what we saw. Just a few yards into the woods from the camp we came across a sight that I shall never forget. Several German girls had been raped and killed; some of them had been strung up by the feet and their throats slit. Some Americans had told me about this, but I had found it too difficult to believe. We paused to say a few prayers. When we arrived at what was once the beautiful little city of Neu-brandenburg, I had the feeling that I was looking upon the end of the world and Judgment Day. I almost expected to see the Four Horsemen of the Apocalypse come galloping towards us

Most of the buildings were still burning, and the streets were piled high with the debris of fallen walls. A large group of Germans, men, women, and children were clearing the main street under guard of a Russian girl. Other Russian girls were directing the traffic of the tanks and armored vehicles moving through the city. Bodies in the streets were ignored, unless they were in the way and obstructed traffic. In places the stench of burnt flesh was horrible. The old priest said nothing, but he would sigh deeply now and then when we met some new horror. He seemed to me at the time as a sort of a symbol of the Church in a devastated world as he lifted his cassock to climb over the debris, and as he stopped by each body to say a short prayer.

We finally arrived at the church rectory and went in. The house had been partly destroyed by fire, and completely wrecked inside. The priest's two sisters, both nuns, and his mother and father had come to him for protection. The priest and his father were sitting on the steps, and were obviously in the state of extreme shock. The women were huddled together on a couch. One of the sisters spoke to the French priest, and told him that the three women had been violated by a group of Russian soldiers, and that their brother and his father had been forced to watch. The French priest asked them if there was anything he could do, though I doubted whether there was anything that anyone was able to do. They shook their heads. I judged that they were on the verge of losing their minds; they were certainly beyond tears, and beyond receiving any expressions of sympathy. A rosary hung from the fingers of the old woman, and as she sat there with her eyes closed I couldn't be sure that she was alive.

We took a different route back to the camp, and we spoke very little on the way. As we were coming up the hill we passed a wagon that had been overturned; it was one of those in which a German family had tried to get away from the Russians. The family had been killed, as was evidenced by the fresh dirt covering a space of the ditch by the wagon; I would say that there were five or six buried there. A German shepherd dog was lying by the wagon, and though we tried to coax him to get up and come with us, he only looked up at us as dogs do when they have been beaten. Looters had already gone through the family possessions. They hadn't bothered to take a little doll that lay among the scattered things, nor had they taken the old family Bible, which the French priest picked up and looked into. The Bible had several First Communion and Confirmation pictures pasted in, and there were many many names under the headings of baptisms, marriages, and deaths. My friend really looked his years now. He had always been so cheerful and pleasant, with a young man's optimistic outlook on life, but now the long walk of the day and the horrible things we had seen made him look worn, old, and tired of life. I was very glad when we got back to the camp, for I was afraid that the old French priest was ill.

Every Russian soldier receives a ration of vodka every day, and some of them had been able to find some German liquor too, so the majority of them were pretty drunk most of the time. While in this condition some of them had taken groups of Americans into the woods and had stripped them of all their valuables. Especially did they prize the American wrist watches. Then they forced Americans to dig their latrines. Finally, several Russian soldiers came into the barracks where we had our sick, and forced our men to drink vodka with them, and demanded all their cigarettes. What I feared more than anything else was that some American might bust a Russian on the nose, and that the Russians, undisciplined as they were, might turn a machine-gun loose on the Americans. We had come too long a way to lose men now. I went down to see the Russian Colonel who was in charge of the camp, but found that he was drunk too. We were beginning to feel much less secure under the Russians than we had under the Germans, and were wondering what we could do about it.

On the 2nd of May an American Colonel, who had been in a Belgian camp near Berlin, arrived at the camp and took command of the American compound. He was astounded at the treatment we were receiving from the Russians. He protested vigorously, but it seemed that front line troops in the Russian army just weren't expected to be disciplined troops, and the danger to our sick and wounded became critical. On the 4th of May an American Captain drove up to the camp in a jeep. He received a rousing welcome from the men, for they thought that he would be leading trucks in to take us back to the American lines, from where, we felt sure, we could almost see the Statue of Liberty. However, the Captain was on a special mission and had a Russian and a German interpreter with him. The Colonel asked the Captain to take me back to the American lines with him, so that I could explain our situation to someone who could do something about it. The Colonel had strictly forbidden any American to leave the camp, for such were General Eisenhower's orders. But each day a couple of dozen would light out on their own towards the American lines, which were about a hundred and fifty miles away. The whole American compound was becoming quite surly, and real trouble with the Russians seemed almost inevitable.

Once on the road, the Captain told me what his mission was. He had been sent in to pick up a German scientist before the Russians reached him. The German was a man of considerable importance, and the Captain was determined that nothing was going to stop him from doing what he was sent to do. The roads were terribly congested, with thousands upon thousand of liberated Poles and Serbs and French and Italians struggling to get back home. Sometimes the procession moved only a couple of miles a day, and sometimes it would be hopelessly stalled for hours. Every conceivable kind of contraption was used for transportation, and dead horses and dead humans lay uncovered along the road, with no one bothering to cover them. The Captain would sometimes leave the road and take to the fields, for the congested traffic was often impossible to cope with. We arrived at Neustre-litz, about forty miles south of Neu-brandenburg, and went directly to the address of the German that the Captain was after. The German lived in a first floor apartment, and after rapping at the door for some time we finally let ourselves in through a window.

We waited in the apartment for about four hours before our man finally showed up. The Captain stood behind the door as he inserted his key into the lock, and when the German stepped in he felt a forty-five stuck in his back. The interpreter told the German to get into the American uniform that had been brought along for this purpose. As the German complied he was told that he was going back to the American lines with us. He was greatly relieved at that, and said that he would be glad to co-operate in every way. I must confess that I was getting quite a schoolboy thrill out of my accidental participation in this adventure. But the whole thing impressed me as being even more "corny" than the usual Hollywood script.

The Captain thought that we might more quickly reach the American lines by going south through Berlin. However, when we arrived on the outskirts of that city it became clear to us that we would not get very far that way before our German friend would be interrogated by the Russian police, who were stopping and questioning everyone. We turned around and headed northwest towards the Elbe river. Our first night we did not stop to sleep, but caught what catnaps we could by taking turns driving. The second night we stopped at an abandoned farm house, and hid the jeep in the barn. The German slept soundly all night, probably the first restful night he had had since the Russians took his little city. I was glad to see as we went through the towns that few if any had been as badly mauled and burned as had Neu-brandenburg.

On the third day we met a group of ten American airmen who had been prisoners, and were now trying to get to the American lines. They had been having a rough time of it, and were mighty hungry. The Captain had a case of C rations in the jeep, and if this much maligned ration was never appreciated before it certainly was now. The Captain then stopped a large wagon that liberated Poles were using to get home in, and he hooked the wagon on to the back of the jeep. I protested taking the wagon from the Poles, but the Captain said that he would have a better chance of getting the German scientist back to the American lines if he were mixed in with these aircorps men, for as we approached the American lines Russian interrogation officers got tougher and tougher and passes were required. With only four of us in the jeep, the Captain explained to me, each of us would likely be questioned; but with a wagonload of men probably only himself and whoever was driving the jeep would be questioned. I felt very sorry for the Poles, but they were not as disheartened as I had expected they would be; apparently nothing could spoil their joy at their liberation.

We spent three days covering the last seventy miles of Russian-occupied territory. Every ten miles or so we were stopped by the suspicious Russian police. The Captain and myself would always go together to see the local Commandant to get a pass. This procedure usually involved drinking several vodka highballs with the Commandant, and discussing the various aspects of the war. We were very liberal with our compliments to the Red army's role, which always pleased the Russians very much, and the American army was always complimented in return. The British part in the war was generally treated with scorn by all Russians. We dared not refuse to toast Uncle Joe, President Roosevelt, General Eisenhower, and innumerable Russian general officers; failure to respond to a toast is the gravest of social errors and an insult to a Russian. After the third or fourth such affair I wasn't quite sure whom I was toasting; my stomach felt like a ball of fire.

When we got within ten miles of Ludwiglust we were stopped again. What a headache it was to get a pass from the Commandant there. The Captain and I went up to see him about seven o'clock in the evening, but the Captain excused himself after about an hour, and left me with the interpreter to try to get the pass from the Russian Major.

The Major had a couple of Russian girls with him, one of whom could speak a bit of English and seemed to be the one who made the decisions for him. Liquor of all kinds was flowing freely, and the table was loaded with fried chicken; very well cooked, too, I might add. The Major was almost too drunk to sign his name to the pass, which he was quite willing to grant. But the girl kept telling him not to, for she said she didn't trust me. She gave me quite a going over in broken English, and said that she knew that I was not telling the truth. I never felt so inclined to strike a woman in my life, but restrained myself with the help of the chicken and perpetual toasts that the Major kept proposing. Finally, for no apparent reason, the girl gave the Major a pencil and told him to sign the pass, and my faith in the essential goodness of womankind was restored. She let me know, however, that I wasn't fooling her a bit. It was now after eleven p.m. Four hours had been spent with that weird couple and their chicken and liquor. I felt definitely the worse for the wear, and was afraid now that the Captain and the others might have gone without me, presuming that I had been unable to get the pass. They were still waiting, however, and I breathed a grateful sigh of relief.

We finally arrived at Ludwiglust, and were stopped for the last time at the bridge over the canal which separated the Russians from the American sector. The Russian guard stopped us there and demanded another pass to get to the American side; but the American guard started a discussion with the Russian guard, and while they were talking the Captain stepped on the gas and over we went to the American side. The guard became quite excited and shouted for us to come back, but Uncle Joe himself couldn't have accomplished that. The 82nd Airborne

Division was occupying this sector, and we found that besides being one of the best fighting outfits in the world they were the most hospitable. They also gave us the great news that this was VE day — that the war in Europe was over at last.

The next day, after a big steak dinner, we were sent to Ninth Army Headquarters at Hildesheim. There I was able to contact the Ninth Army G2 and tell him the whole story of the situation at Stalag II-A. He said that General Eisenhower had had reports similar to that from other Stalags, and that negotiations were under way to evacuate American prisoners of war immediately. The Captain turned his German scientist over to the G2, and we parted. The G2 fixed me up with a clean uniform and that evening I flew to Paris.

The plane that flew us to Paris had six liberated Frenchmen aboard, and they could scarcely control their joy at going home after those five long years of imprisonment. At the first sight of the Eiffel Tower they let out a whoop and brought forth three bottles of wine from someplace. They insisted (though it didn't take too much insisting) that all of us drink a toast to Paris. I had often heard that Paris was loved like a mother by all Frenchmen, and I was quite moved to see these emaciated home-sick men feast their tear-dimmed eyes upon their beloved city. I wondered if any other city in the world is as dear to her native sons.

Our landing was delayed for about half an hour by the crashing of an English plane on the runway sometime that morning. We continued to fly over the city, and the Frenchmen pointed out the famous landmarks for us. When we finally came down we inquired about the plane that had crashed and was still smoking at the end of one of the runways. We were told that the two pilots and most of the thirty-two liberated British prisoners aboard had died in the crash. The next day I said Mass for them, though I had looked forward to and planned a Mass of thanksgiving for my own liberation.

In Paris I was given some pay and a seventy-two-hour pass before I would entrain for Le Havre. I met a group of men from my outfit in Paris, and the way they welcomed me and treated me made me realize how much I had missed them. We spent the evening discussing the Regiment and all the changes that had taken place in it. I wanted to go back with them to Rheims where the Regiment was again stationed, but my orders stated that I was to report to Camp Lucky Strike near Le Havre, and would be shipped back to the States as soon as possible. This wasn't such a hard order to take, however, as I was distinctly and completely home-sick. I sent a couple of notes back with these GIs to the Regimental CO and to Chaplain Engle telling them to be sure to hold my place in the Regiment open for me, for I fully intended to return to it. My short stay in Paris was very pleasant, and I had a fine room assigned to me in the best hotel in the city. I spent most of three days visiting the famous churches and other places of interest, but the greatest pleasure was simply walking as a free man among free men.

Camp Lucky Strike was quite a place — a tent city housing the thousands of prisoners of war who kept pouring in from all parts of Europe. They went all out there to fatten us up before we returned to the States. We were given the opportunity to enjoy the luxury of a shower, and new uniforms were issued. The meals were tremendous, and were prepared better than any army food that I have ever had. You could have five meals a day if you could eat them, with chicken and steak being the chief items on menus which invariably finished with pie a la mode. Eggnogs were passed out between meals. This may seem hard for you to believe, but I gained about thirty pounds in the two weeks that I was there. A couple of other priests who had been prisoners in other camps were at Lucky Strike too, and we all had a great time together.

We sailed May 26, and the voyage was rough but pleasant. The whole boat seemed intoxicated with the joy of going home. I celebrated Mass every day, and the attendance was very good. Apparently most of the men were mighty grateful to the power that brought them through. I doubt if many will ever forget their experiences or the Providence that made it possible for them to return to their families.

I think that I shall always hesitate to believe or to disbelieve war stories, for I know that GIs sometimes tell whoppers, but I also know that the incredible does happen. The past year and a half is already beginning to seem more like a dream than reality, and I suppose in time that I shall almost be able to forget it entirely. Right now I am quite confused and bewildered and staggered by the terrific price of this war in human life and suffering. History alone will establish, I suppose, whether the good that comes out of it all will bear some proportion to the tremendous cost. About all I can think of now is the peaceful and happy life of a parish assistant in some little Iowa town — busy with the school children, with Catholic Youth groups, with confessions, with daily Mass, and with preparing the Sunday sermon. God willing, that's for me.

PART IV: HOME

CHAPTER X: AFTERTHOUGHTS

Well, it does seem good to be back in the uniform of the Church. I never realized before how comfortable and practical the black suit and the Roman collar really are. Besides, I never could tie a decent four-in-hand. Taking off the Army uniform and putting on the clerical garb seemed almost like a ceremony marking the end of one period of my life and the beginning of another, and I had the feeling quite like the one I experienced in taking the step forward during the reception of the subdiaconate, salva reverentia.

Although all the Catholic chaplains I have talked to since returning from overseas are more than anxious to get out of the service, not one regretted having served in the Army, and everyone of them felt that combat experience especially had benefitted him a great deal. Combat truly was a perfect laboratory for a priest's study and work. There human nature was exposed for dissection and analysis… all the artificialities and superficialities of civilian life were cut away, and there remained nothing but bedrock character, or sometimes, sadly enough, the almost total lack of character. Family position, social status, money, influence — these were mighty helpless assets at the front. But the one factor that did follow the men wherever they went, the one thing that stood by them during the darkest hours, and gave them the help and the courage they needed was the discipline and training they had received at home. Yes, as I leave the Army, that is the one conviction I bring with me stronger than all others, the importance of home training. Of course, I believed it before, but I could never have had it so graphically illustrated in civilian life. Our religion, with its wise emphasis upon inculcating the sense of duty and obligation in children, gives them the moral stability that makes for ordered, happy lives, worthy members of Holy Mother Church and useful citizens of our country.

Several of us priests together were separated from the Army about two weeks ago at Fort Sheridan. About 1200 enlisted men and officers were separated on the same day, which happened to be Sunday. The chapel was packed for Mass. This was to be my last Mass as an Army chaplain, and the last for these men as soldiers. As I faced them for the sermon I couldn't help but feel that I was going to miss my khaki-clad congregations. Soldiers are something of a paradox. Their faults and their sins are apparent; yet their virtues are many. They swagger and boast; yet they seem to have a depth of humility that reveals itself to a chaplain in so many ways. Their language is coarse and crude, and their humor often disgusting; but their confessions are frank and their purpose of amendment sincere. The monotony and routine of Army life seem to make them hard and sometimes even cruel to one another; but their sense of humor, their kindnesses, and their amazing bursts of generosity to each other more than make up for moments of meanness and pettiness. It is difficult to leave a group of men like that, men with whom you have lived for several years more intimately than with brothers. Catholic men have a tendency to glamorize their chaplain away beyond his merits. No amount of Army regulations, circulars, and bulletins could get them to call their priest "Chaplain" instead of "Father." You can understand why I began to regret that this was to be my last sermon to soldiers, and I had a hunch that I would miss them more and more as time went on. The thought that I tried to put over to them that day went something like this:

"When a man comes into the Army he stands before a delegated authority and with his right hand raised he swears to respect and obey all legitimate orders of lawful superiors, and to protect and defend his country from all enemies foreign and domestic. Now you are about to be released from the Army and from many of the special obligations that were yours as soldiers. But in a very real sense army life is nothing new to Catholics. You have been in the army since the day you were baptized — in the army of Jesus Christ. At your baptism and through your godparents you swore to obey all orders of Jesus and His Church, and you vowed to protect and to defend the sanctuary of your immortal soul from all enemies foreign and domestic. As the waters of baptism were poured over your forehead you were clothed in the spotless uniform of sanctifying grace; you were a rookie in God's army — weak, untrained, incapable of combat yet, it was true. But your parents and the good Sisters in school would teach you, Holy Communion and confession would strengthen you, and Confirmation would establish you as a fighting soldier of Christ.

"The enemy? Not the Axis of Germany, Italy, and Japan, but an enemy far more crafty, far more resourceful. Your enemy and God's is the Axis of the world, the flesh, and the devil... the world with all its tinsel and baubles, its false front, its sham and hypocrisy; the flesh with its poisoned delights, its insipid pleasures, its sensuality and insobriety; the devil with his hatred and his greed, envy, avarice, and sloth. That is the enemy that you are duty-bound to fight; that is the enemy that has never got over the crushing defeat it suffered in the first clash of arms with Jesus on the battlefield of Calvary.

"But proper weapons of warfare are necessary in order to win the war against the enemies of your soul. You might as soon expect to stop a Tiger tank with a pea-shooter, or shoot down Japanese Zero planes with sling shots, as to fight the world, the flesh, and the devil without the proper weapons. No matter how well disposed you may be, or how strong a will you have, or how determined you are; it makes no difference how favorable your home life and environment are or what material advantages you may have; unless you use the weapons our Blessed Lord has given to you, and use them according to his instructions, you are doomed to inevitable defeat. Jesus has given you these weapons you need, and as your Commander He guarantees that if you use them properly and as instructed you will win out. These weapons are prayer (daily prayer and frequent ejaculations), the Rosary, the Stations of the Cross, and, most effective of all, frequent confession and Communion. These are your machine guns, your tanks, your heavy artillery, and your dive-bombers, and they have proved their effectiveness in every battle of life as all the saints in Heaven and devout Catholics on earth will testify.

"Combat was a spiritual rest period for all of us. When you were lying in a muddy fox-hole, miserable and scared, prayer came easy, didn't it? When you were on an outpost at night, and every rustle of the wind in the bushes conjured up in your imagination an enemy only a few feet away, you weren't planning a drunken brawl for the next week-end. When 88s zeroed in on your sector, and tree-bursts were throwing shrapnel in every direction, you had no difficulty in banishing impure thoughts and desires. The peace and quiet of home and the real values in life were what you longed for, weren't they? You got a lot of comfort out of your Rosary when you had a chance to say part of a decade at the front, didn't you? I believe you made a number of promises to God then, didn't you? Have you forgotten those promises? God hasn't. Are you as sincere about them now as when you made them? God is. Yes, combat was a spiritual rest period; you felt close to God, and it was a mighty comforting feeling.

"But now you are going back home, and, though this may sound strange to you, you are going to be in a real battle. The opportunity and the temptation to break every promise to God that you ever made is going to be thrust at you from every side. Your family will be overjoyed to have you home, and the old gang will welcome you back, and your pastor will be delighted to see you; don't fail to call upon him. But still, no matter how small your home town may be or how large, the world, the flesh, and the devil will be there, urging you to compromise, to shirk your duties as a soldier of Christ, to shed the uniform of sanctifying grace, to go over to the enemy. This is not a mere figure of speech. You must know by now that the real battles of life have always been fought, not on French soil, nor German, nor Italian; not in Europe, Asia, or Africa; but in the souls of men like yourself.

"There is one saboteur of your soul more dangerous than all others. It is discouragement. Discouragement can infiltrate and undermine God's grace, if you let it. Discouragement alone can defeat a Catholic. You have before you the glorious example of Jesus Christ, and you have behind you, perhaps, a lifetime of miserable failures. Urging you onward and upward are the teachings of the Church and the examples of the saints; holding you back and dragging you downward are the consciousness of your own weakness and the sins of the past. Yesterday's resolutions gave promise of real progress; today's failures teach you that you are still a pretty weak human being. With Saint Paul you feel like crying out, 'The good that I would I do not, and the evil that I would not, that I do. Unhappy man that I am, who shall deliver me from the body of this death?' And then Saint Paul's answer to his own question comes ringing down through the ages, as true now as it was then and always will be, true for you and for me and for every man, woman, and child on the face of the globe, 'Who shall deliver me from the body of this death? The grace of God, which is in Christ Jesus, our Lord!' and you get this grace, men, principally through the Holy Sacrifice of the Mass, and through the sacraments of Penance and Holy Eucharist. Stay close to these and you will always be a strong and true soldier of Christ, worthy to share in His glory on the Day of Victory!"

Just before leaving Fort Sheridan as a civilian again, I received a letter from Chaplain Engle. You remember, the Protestant chaplain in our Regiment, a good fellow and very sincere. The Regiment is at Berchtesgaden, Hitler's old hangout. Chaplain Engle writes that Colonel Ewell was seriously wounded in the foot, but that they might be able to avoid an amputation. He had walked into the open to get a better view of a couple of German tanks about 600 yards away. One of the tanks let go at him, and when he was asked why he hadn't stayed under cover he replied, "Why, I've read those lousy Krauts' artillery field manuals, and they say that an artillery piece is never to fire at individual enemy personnel, but only when several of the enemy are together." It seems that the Germans weren't playing according to the book. Chaplain Engle, commenting upon my affinity for water and the fact that on almost every jump I landed in a river, a canal, or a lake, closed with this observation, "I've always felt that the frequency of your immersions was a Providential sign that you should have been a Baptist."

After separation I rode to Chicago to get a black suit. I was unable to find one in the ten or twelve clothing stores that I went into; one of the salesmen said that during the war they had been forbidden to sell them, because the OPA found that they were being retailored into tuxedos. I got my old black suits out of the mothballs in Neola and went to Des Moines to report to the Bishop for assignment. I shall never forget Bishop Bergan's welcome when I returned from overseas. It was the most genuine and sincerely warm reception that I have ever received outside my own home. Pie is one of those rare individuals who combine the dignity and authority of a responsible position with a kind, witty, and humble personality. Msgr. Lyons, rector of the Cathedral, invited me to stay there at the rectory until the Bishop decided what my assignment was to be. I spent a very restful and enjoyable four days.

You recall that in the letter I wrote you on my way back to the States I said that all I could think of was the peaceful and happy life of a parish assistant in some little Iowa town, busy with the school children, CYO, and parish duties. Well, that is precisely the assignment that I received. Westphalia is scarcely discernible on a state map, but it is a well-known little town. In the December issue of Fortune magazine there is a very interesting article about Westphalia and about Fr. Duren (the same name as the hospital chaplain in Normandy, if you recall). Fr. Duren has established the community on a co-operative basis, and there are five points to the program: Religion,

Education, Recreation, Commerce, and Credit. The fundamental principle by which these things are coordinated was not original with Fr. Duren, and he is the first to give the credit to the real Author of the Westphalia idea; our Blessed Lord: "Build the Kingdom of God great... and all these things shall be added unto you." It sounds very idealistic and impractical, doesn't it? But Fr. Duren has made it work.

The village and the surrounding country are solidly Catholic, and the Church is the center of everyone's life. For example, on Sunday the entire congregation sings the Gregorian Mass, and almost everyone receives Holy Communion weekly. On All Souls day everyone attended the three Masses and the procession to the cemetery. Education is the second point of the program, and Westphalia has a fine school and a splendid group of Franciscan sisters as teachers. They are the happiest and jolliest group of sisters that I have ever seen; perhaps that is why they do such a superior job of teaching. There are adult study groups too, and these are surprisingly well attended. I am the monitor of one of these groups and find the work fascinating. Recreation is one of the main points of the program, and there is scarcely an evening that does not have something going on in the school auditorium and gymnasium: basketball games, dramatics, Four H Club demonstrations, dances, etc. Fr. Duren has built up a splendid school band too. It is really amusing to see some of the little children blowing on a horn for all they are worth, trying to beat time with a foot that doesn't reach the floor, concentrated on the music sheet and trying to keep up. The total effect, though, is very good. Father has established a club house for the men, too. There they can meet their neighbors, talk over the day's events, or play a game of pool or cards. The Co-operative store is the big contribution under Commerce. Last year it did a $125,000 business, underselling by a good deal the prices charged in the nearby towns for the same items. It saves the farmers and townspeople the ten-mile trip to the nearest town, saves them money on the goods they buy, and returns a dividend to them each year for their investment in the Co-operative. The Co-operative Credit and Loan Association formed by Fr. Duren enables the people to borrow at small interest, and to repay at their convenience. The people themselves have invested about $140,000 in this, and of course draw interest on it. Westphalia is one little country town that is not losing its young men, who return from the service, to the cities. The people are co-operative and helpful to one another. They support the Church generously and intelligently. For example, each farmer gives to the Church one acre of corn for every fifty acres he has. They haul the corn in to the cribs behind the school, get together and shell it, sell it, and turn the check over to Fr. Duren. As you may have gathered, Fr. Duren is quite a fellow, big as a house, and as congenial a priest as I have ever known, with unlimited enthusiasm for the Westphalia Plan. Yes, Westphalia is some place. There is a sign by the road, as you enter the village, reading: "Where the world is at its best... Westphalia." I believe it.

In your last letter you asked whether I was still bothered by the memory of combat experiences. No, not particularly. I am kept busy enough not to let it bother me much. A good deal of it, though, I don't want to forget. In the last two weeks I have received a couple of dozen letters from 501st men; the Regiment is going to have an annual reunion and I am eagerly looking forward to it. I haven't heard whether Colonel Kinnard came through the

Bastogne engagement without injury or not. He and Colonel Ewell will always stand out in my mind as perfect officers and gentlemen. They were classmates at West Point. Everywhere you hear severe criticism of West Point officers, and the general impression is that they didn't carry their weight, and were shown up badly by other officers. Of course, I didn't know very many West Point officers, but those I did know, by and large, were very superior men. Major General Taylor, our Division Commander, General McAuliffe (of "Nuts" fame), Colonels Kinnard, Ewell, Farrell, Majors Roberts and Saunders, all West Point men, were a splendid group of officers and most co-operative with the chaplain's work.

By the way, I am to give a Radio talk — sort of a memorial address — on May first. It is to be sponsored by the American Legion. I should like very much to have you read it, and let me have your honest reaction. I am anxious that it should really carry the thought about which I feel very strongly. It is entitled "One Year After," — and reads in part as follows.

"The hard and difficult thing about war for those at the front were the long days that went by when none of us could raise his eyes beyond the next foxhole or above the next rise of muddy ground. Friends died and were taken away, and we were all too busy with the work at hand to think about them very long. A little later, during a lull in battle, we were able to assemble in formation at a military cemetery for services. The services were very sincere but short, for our duties called us back to the front almost immediately. Today, however, we can pause for a little while and think.

"Like every GI there are many things about war that I am anxious to forget. I am anxious to forget the necessary sordidness and cruelties of battle. I want to forget the mud and the muck and the mire, the painful days and the endless nights. I want to forget the sickening sensation of fear. But like every GI too, there are many things that I want to remember. I want to remember the innate sense of humor of the American boy, that reservoir of good-nature that seems to be a by-product of his native courage and optimism... his incredible ability to joke and laugh under the most severe trials...

"But there is something else that I want to remember. I want to remember such boys as Nathan Miller, a Jewish boy, who was literally cut in two by machine-gun fire when he walked within twenty-five yards of a German tank and knocked it out with his bazooka. I want to remember boys like Phillip Levitt, a Protestant boy, who died in my arms saying the Lord's prayer. I want to remember boys like Aloysius Furdak, who stopped a sniper's bullet when he was in the act of bandaging a wounded boy's leg. I want to remember literally hundreds of boys whom it was my very great privilege to be near in their last hour. I want to remember, too, some 288,000 little white crosses that now dot foreign fields — each one representing a priceless treasure of our country. Those simple little crosses have nothing on them but a name, a serial number, the date of death, and a dog-tag nailed there that jingles in a rather melancholy manner at night when the wind blows. We must never think of war casualties in terms of statistics; every one of us must remember that each cross and each star of David represents not only the supreme sacrifice of a fine young man, but it must also remind us of the tears of a mother and father and the empty place in a home that can never be filled, though his memory is perpetually cherished in the photograph on the family piano and the Purple Heart beside the photograph. The feeling I am sure you share with me is one of inadequacy. How, we ask ourselves, can the laying of wreaths, the parades, the heads bowed in reverence, indicate either their sacrifice or our sentiments?

"Let us for a moment, in our mind's eye, draw aside the veil that separates us from these boys who gave their lives for our country. See them standing before us, row after row of them. There's the boy that used to deliver your paper, remember? And there is Tom Jones, who made such a name for himself in high school athletics. And there is Marvin Peters who did so well supporting his mother after his father died. And there — well, they all look familiar: happy, energetic American boys full of the vigor of youth. What now do they expect of us? What can we do for them now that they are dead? Do they ask for praise?... grandeur?... eloquence? I think not. Do they ask to have their deeds eulogized? No, I think they would resent any attempt on our part to place halos about their heads. But if they could look down upon our country today and see us working together for the ideals upon which our country was founded; if they could see us co-operating with one another in the spirit of understanding and Christian charity; if they could see us of every station in life, all working together, and ready and eager, each one of us, to make any personal sacrifice necessary; if those boys looking down could see that, then figuratively speaking, they could polish up their boots, and shine up their brass, and with shoulders back each one could strut down the golden streets of Paradise (as we have often seen them strut down our streets) and he could nudge an old-timer up there, and, pointing down at us, say with pardonable pride:

'That's my country; those are my people, and what I died for was worth dying for.'

"There is a dangerous tendency in all of us to accept the great principles embodied in our Constitution as inalienable rights about which we need do nothing. That right to life, for example, if it be inalienable, belongs to every person in the world, be he Chinese, Hungarian, Italian, Greek, Dutch, or African. But millions of lives in these countries are being threatened by starvation. If we really believe in the right to life, you and I must approve our country's sharing its food resources; we must do more. There is a personal obligation. I must tighten my belt and you must tighten yours. We believe in the principle of liberty; then we are obligated to demand that right for peoples of other lands, even though our own wartime Allies may seem to refuse them that right. If we fail in this our boys have fought in vain, for it was in defense of that right that this country went to war. The pursuit of happiness is our natural right and we almost take it for granted. But this right is being attacked in the United States of America, the land of the free, as well as in foreign countries. Strangely enough, certain groups, such as the Ku Klux Kian, dare to rear their ugly serpentine heads again and to sink their deadly fangs of racial discrimination and religious bigotry into the war-weary public.

"Our obligations and our debt of gratitude to the dead of World War I and of World War II cannot be paid simply by accepting in theory the ideals for which they died, and then continuing to live blindly selfish lives. The men in the service didn't perhaps, philosophize deeply about the cause of the war, but they did know that they were fighting for a way of life that they loved. The sceptic and the scoffer may rant and rave about false causes of this last war, about money-mad war-mongers, about British Imperialism, and about any number of other things. I have no original answer to that. I can but point out our plain duty by appealing to one of the gentlest and kindest men who ever lived. Somehow, his words, after more than eighty years, seem singularly appropriate here today:

It is for us, the living, rather to be dedicated here to the unfinished work which they who fought here have thus far so nobly advanced. It is rather for us to be here dedicated to the great task remaining before us; that from these honored dead we take increased devotion to that cause for which they gave the last full measure of devotion; that we here highly resolve that these dead shall not have died in vain; that this nation, under God, shall have a new birth of freedom; and that government of the people, by the people, for the people shall not perish from the earth.

"Indeed it is proper that we be dedicated again, and that every aspect of American life be dedicated to the great task that lies before us; that labor and capital give and receive mutual respect for each other's rights, the welfare of the nation standing-before either; that radio and the press, entering as they do into the very sanctuary of the American home, be a force for wholesome intelligent living rather than stoop to satisfy the morbidly curious; that the motion picture industry recognize its tremendous influence upon the youth of our country, and that it seek to elevate rather than to degrade; that all of us recognize that there is a greater God than the dollar; that it is more important to make people better than to make cars better; and that we must expect that America bless God, before we can expect that God bless America. These are our duties and our mandate from above.

"Yes, our departed comrades-in-arms, you who died that we might live, and that the world might have a new birth of freedom; yes, Tom and Jack and Larry and Pete and Frank and Henry and Joe, Fred and Bill and Clyde and Mike and Dick and Steve, and every last one of you who fought and bled and died: we do solemnly pledge by all that is sacred to your memory, 'that you shall not have died in vain.'"

A NOTE TO THE READER

WE HOPED YOU LOVED THIS BOOK. IF YOU DID, PLEASE LEAVE A REVIEW ON AMAZON TO LET EVERYONE ELSE KNOW WHAT YOU THOUGHT.

WE WOULD ALSO LIKE TO THANK OUR SPONSORS **WWW.DIGITALHISTORYBOOKS.COM** WHO MADE THE PUBLICATION OF THIS BOOK POSSIBLE.

WWW.DIGITALHISTORYBOOKS.COM PROVIDES A WEEKLY NEWSLETTER OF THE BEST DEALS IN HISTORY AND HISTORICAL FICTION.

SIGN UP TO THEIR NEWLSETTER TO FIND OUT MORE ABOUT THEIR LATEST DEALS.

Made in the USA
Middletown, DE
10 March 2020

86153527R00097